DISCOVER
CORNWALL
FROM ABOVE

Contents

MYRIAD
LONDON

North Cornwall

Cornwall – or Kernow in Cornish – is England's most south-western county and has the best climate too. But the superlatives don't stop there. It is the county with the longest coastline in the UK: 433 miles (697km), including 146 miles (235km) of Heritage coast. It also has some of the best beaches – over 300 – so it is no surprise that Cornwall attracts five million visitors every year, most coming from within the UK. They come to explore the county's natural beauty which dates from the dawn of time, for the pleasure of the seaside resorts and to be inspired by 21st century design. Cornwall has its own history, food and language, which is being actively promoted. According to local folklore the devil never ventured into Cornwall for fear of ending up in a pasty!

Bude The resort of Bude stands at the mouth of the river Neet on Cornwall's north coast. Its name comes from "Bede Haven", meaning harbour of holy men. The town's fortunes changed with the opening of the Bude canal (left) in the 1820s. The canal was first mooted in 1774 to link the Bristol and English Channels via the river Tamar, but in the end only 35.5 miles (57km) were completed. Its main purpose was agricultural: to transport lime-rich sand to the hinterland where it was used to improve the quality of the soil. Bude developed as a tourist resort with the arrival of the railway in 1898 and the opening of the branch line from Holsworthy – a subsequent casualty of the Beeching cuts in 1966. Visitors were drawn to the area by the fresh Atlantic air and the wide-open scenery.

Crooklets Beach In the 1950s surfers discovered the delights of Bude's Crooklets Beach (above). The broad, west-facing expanse of sand of this Blue Flag beach runs from Wrangles Rock to the north and Barrel Rock in the south. The variety of the waves caters for surfers of all levels. The Bude Surf Club was a founder member in 1955 of the Surf Life Saving Association of Great Britain. A more recent event in Bude has become known locally as "the Bude Boom". At about 11.50 on 26 October 2006 there was a loud and unexplained noise over the town, parts of which experienced property damage. Subsequent suggestions of a possible cause include an RAF aircraft breaking the sound barrier or a meteor exploding out in the stratosphere.

Boscastle The village of Boscastle (above) grew up around its medieval harbour and clings to the slopes of the valley where the rivers Valency and Jordan meet. The name is derived from the now ruined Bottreaux Castle, built in Norman times by the Botterel family. Protected by Pennally Point, Boscastle offers the only natural harbour on this stretch of coast. The two harbour walls were built in 1584 by Sir Richard Grenville. The harbour and much of the surrounding area are now owned by the National Trust. In the afternoon of 16 August 2004 disaster struck Boscastle. After a period of very heavy rain, a flash flood estimated at about 440 million gallons of water raged through the village. Luckily no lives were lost but there was extensive damage. The local council, the National Trust and English Heritage have since been at pains to maintain the character of the village during the restoration work. One of Boscastle's attractions is the Museum of Witchcraft, which houses one of the world's most extensive collections of witchcraft-related items. Established in 1960, the museum is open daily from Easter to Halloween.

Tintagel Head (left, above and right) is one of Cornwall's most iconic sights. Here stand the ruins of Tintagel Castle, the legendary birthplace of King Arthur and home of the wizard Merlin. There have been fortifications on this spot since the Iron Age, but the ruins we see today date from the 13th century, when the castle was home to the Earls of Cornwall. At low tide it is possible to walk through Merlin's cave, once the favourite hiding place of smugglers. Tintagel's Old Post Office is a 14th century stone house, used as a district post office for 50 years in the 19th century. It is now owned by the National Trust. At St Paul's church is the unique and poignant Miscarriage and Infant Loss Memorial Book, where parents can record the loss of a baby from conception to three years old. To explore Tintagel Head, it is best to park in nearby Tintagel village.

Port Isaac

The narrow winding streets of the fishing village of Port Isaac (above) situated between Wadebridge and Camelford, all lead down to its pretty harbour through which slate, coal, wood and pottery once passed. The village dates from the Middle Ages. With its slate-fronted houses and whitewashed cottages, it is a favourite with film and television programme-makers. The film *Oscar and Lucinda* was shot here as was the ITV series *Doc Martin* starring Martin Clunes and the TV series *Poldark*.

Seven Bays for Seven Days

To the west of the Camel estuary and Padstow Bay lies the coastline (right) sometimes described as "seven bays for seven days", punctuated by the headland of Trevose Head. Just visible above the caravan park in the bottom of the picture above is Polverton or Mother Ivey's Bay, then the broad sweep of Harlyn Bay and, beyond, Trevone Bay protected by the cliffs of Gunver Head.

The Camel Estuary The estuary of the river Camel stretches about five miles (8km) from the coast inland to Wadebridge. The river's name is said to come from the Cornish word for "crooked one". On the western shore sits the town of Padstow (above). It was once considered the ecclesiastical capital of Cornwall because of the nearby monastery founded by St Petroc, who came from Ireland in the 6th century. Today Padstow is a bustling fishing port and holiday resort, made famous by the restaurateur Rick Stein. From Padstow you can take the Black Tor ferry to the village opposite. Rock (below) is home to more millionaires than anywhere else in Cornwall. It attracts rich and famous visitors, and the town has been dubbed the Kensington of Cornwall and Britain's St Tropez.

Trevose Head The lighthouse at Trevose Head (above) sits on granite cliffs that tower 150ft (46m) over the sea. A lighthouse was first proposed for this spot in 1809 but it only became operational in 1847, and was automated in 1995. It is open to the public on weekdays. The new Trevose Head lifeboat station and slipway (left) opened in August 2006 and houses the Padstow lifeboat.

Treyarnon and Constantine Bays South of Trevose Head lie two more of the "seven bays for seven days". The long stretch of Constantine Bay (right, foreground) is separated from Trevose golf course by sand dunes topped with marram grass. Top quality waves make Constantine Bay a favourite with surfers. The smaller Treyarnon Bay (right, centre) is set in an area of outstanding natural beauty with rock pools and idyllic small coves. To the south of the bay, erosion has produced a series of deep coves. Running right to left are Fox Cove, Warren Cove and Pepper Cove. Trethias Island, separated by a narrow channel, guards the entrance to Treyarnon Bay, and is home to nesting seabirds.

Newquay The town grew up around its fishing harbour which thrived on the humble pilchard until the industry's demise early in the 20th century. The beaches stretching round Newquay Bay became the main attraction for visitors and turned the area into a major holiday destination. The local population of 20,000 swells to 100,000 during the summer months. In recent years surfers of all levels have flocked to Newquay, which proudly claims to be the surfing capital of Britain. Beginners head to the Great Western beach with its smaller surf, while experienced surfers head across the fairways of Newquay golf course to the more exposed Fistral Beach with its rolling Atlantic breakers. Rated one of the best surfing beaches in the UK, Fistral Beach has hosted many national and international surfing competitions. In 2010 it will host the main events in Rescue 2010, the life-saving world championships. Overlooking Fistral Beach with fine views of Towan Head is the Headland Hotel, which has been welcoming visitors including royalty since 1900.

Perranporth Six miles
south-west of the surfing capital
of Bude, Perranporth (left and
above), with its wide open beach
and dependable waves, is also a
favourite with board enthusiasts.
The village's name is Cornish for
St Piran's Port. St Piran is the
patron saint of Cornwall and it
is believed that he founded the
recently discovered church in
Perranporth in the 7th century.
The church of St Piran's
Oratory – often known as "the
lost church" because it was only
unearthed in the 20th century –
is now being excavated and
made accessible to the public.
The author Winston Graham
who wrote the *Poldark* series
of historical novels lived in the
village for many years. His tales
are largely set locally and feature
characters and families involved
in the 18th and 19th century
tin-mining industry. "Hendrawna
Sands" features in the novels as
Perranporth beach. The
Perranzabuloe Folk Museum in
the village is dedicated to the
life and work of the author.

Portreath The village of Portreath (above) about 5 miles north of Redruth, was once a busy port and the present harbour dates from 1760. Ships laden with copper ore would sail over to Swansea in south Wales and return with coal. The first tramway in Cornwall was built in 1809 to bring the copper ore to Portreath from further afield. Now pleasurecraft and fishing boats occupy the harbour and the tramway is a footpath enjoyed by walkers and cyclists.

Godrevy Point This headland (left) facing north into the Atlantic lies about about three miles north-east of the town of Hayle and marks the eastern end of St Ives Bay. Godrevy Island lies about half a mile from the headland and is owned by the National Trust. The lighthouse on the island was erected in 1859 and is said to have inspired Virginia Woolf's novel *To the Lighthouse*. In 1934 the lighthouse was automated, so the island is uninhabited.

West Cornwall

The "granite kingdom" of west Cornwall sits on the Land's End peninsula which runs for 36 miles from St Ives in the north to Penzance and Mount's Bay in the south. The area is a mix of sandy beaches, towering cliffs, desolate moorland and characterful towns and villages. Everywhere there is evidence of the area's industrial heritage of tin and china clay mining. Land's End Visitor's Centre, close to the most westerly point of the English mainland, is a "must see" destination for visitors. Also popular is Penzance, the unofficial "capital" of west Cornwall and St Ives with its fine beaches and cultural atttractions. St Ives quickly developed as a resort when, in 1877, the railway reached the town with the opening of the branch line from St Erth at the head of the Hayle estuary.

St Ives Artists have always been drawn to St Ives by the quality of its light. Early visitors included Sydney Lawrence, Walter Sickert, James Whistler and JMW Turner. The artists' colony of today was founded in 1928 by the Cornish artist Alfred Wallis and his friends Ben Nicholson and Christopher Wood. In 1939 Ben Nicholson and Barbara Hepworth settled in St Ives, along with Naum Gabo, and during the next 15 years St Ives celebrated its golden age. Art galleries abound in the town and in 1993 the second branch of the Tate Gallery outside London opened. The Tate also looks after the nearby Barbara Hepworth museum and sculpture garden. The annual St Ives September festival of art and music is one of the longest running in Britain.

Pendeen Tin Tin has been mined around Pendeen since the beginning of the 18th century. The Geevor mine (right) was one of the last to open; the Levant mine nearby is one of Cornwall's most famous. After production ceased in 1990, the old mine buildings were adapted and the Geevor Tin Mine Heritage Centre opened in August 1993. The centre, where visitors can learn about the mining and processing of tin, is the largest preserved mining centre in Britain.

Long Carn Whirlpool The sea crashes on the rocks below the cliffs between the isolated Porthmoina and Portheras coves (below) forming a whirlpool. Above, the area is rich in Cornish history: close to the path at Trevowhan cliff there are open mine shafts; a little distance inland is the megalithic Boskednan stone circle, also known as the Nine Maidens, which may once have had as many as 22 upright stones.

Land's End The most westerly point in mainland Britain, Land's End (above and right), is still an awe-inspiring sight if somewhat commercialised. The famous signpost showing the distances to New York and John O'Groats is now part of a theme park. Among the visitors are the End-to-Enders, who turn straight round and set off on the 874 mile (1407km) journey to the northernmost point, John O'Groats in Scotland. In 1879 Cornishman Robert Carlyle was the first person to achieve this feat – pushing a wheelbarrow. One and a half miles (2.4km) offshore, the Longships Lighthouse (above) stands guard on Carn Bras, the largest of the Longships Rocks.

Pordennack Point Heading south from Land's End, the beaches of the north Cornish coast give way to a more rugged coastline. In the foreground of the picture above, just offshore, sits the island of Enys Dodnan, famed for its arched rock.

Behind lie the headlands of Pordennack Point, Carn Boel and beyond Mill Bay, Carn Les Boel. Walkers on this stretch of the South West Coast Path are often rewarded by sightings of seabirds including gannets, guillemots and razorbills. Further out to sea you can sometimes catch sight of basking sharks (inset). Together with dolphins, porpoises and grey seals they are attracted to the area by the clear, clean water and abundant supply of food.

Gwennap Head The South West Coast Path is clearly visible as it traces its way across Gwennap Head (above), the most southerly point of the Penwith peninsula. This section is also known as the Penwith Heritage Coast which stretches 33 miles (53km) from St Ives, past Land's End, ending just south of Penzance. An area of outstanding natural beauty, this part of the Cornish coast is a favourite with birdwatchers who come to view marine birds such as skuas, whimbrels, petrels and shearwaters. Gwennap Head also attracts rock climbers who relish the challenge of scaling the granite cliff faces, including the well-known Chair Ladder crag.

Mousehole One of the most picturesque villages in the whole of Cornwall, Mousehole (pronounced "Mowzel") is set around its harbour (left). Many of the houses are built of the local Lamorna granite. Near the harbour a plaque marks the house of Dolly Pentreath, who was reputed to have been the last person to speak only Cornish. She died in 1777. In 1937, Dylan Thomas spent his honeymoon in Mousehole with his wife Caitlin. History does not relate if they ate stargazy pie, the local speciality which has fish heads sticking out through the piecrust.

Penzance Penzance enjoys a sheltered position on Mount's Bay and a warmer climate than anywhere else in Britain. For many years it was overshadowed by nearby Marazion, which was mentioned in the Domesday Book in 1088. Marazion is the oldest chartered town in Britain. But Penzance's fortunes changed: Henry IV granted the town a royal market, Henry VIII allowed it to charge harbour dues and James I made it a borough. Today Penzance has ship repair and dry dock facilities, and its harbour caters for fishing boats and pleasurecraft. The Isles of Scilly Steamship Company runs a seasonal service between Penzance and St Mary's, the largest of the islands.

St Michael's Mount The Cornish cousin of Mont St-Michel in France, St Michael's Mount is linked to Marazion by a causeway that is passable only at mid and low tides. The castle and gardens, home of the St Aubyn family, are maintained by the National Trust.

Predannack Head Above the cliffs at Predannack Head (above) lie a nature reserve and an old airfield, opened in 1941. During the Second World War the RAF flew anti-submarine missions from Predannack airfield over the Bay of Biscay. The airfield is now used by the Royal Navy as a back-up when RNAS Culdrose gets too busy. It is also the base for the Royal Navy School of Fire Fighting and an RAF gliding school. The Lizard national nature reserve covers more than 4,000 acres, has 18 rare plant species and nesting sites for ravens and peregrines.

Cadgwith The pretty fishing village of Cadgwith (right) was first settled in the Middle Ages. Its two beaches are divided by a promontory called the Todden. Big Beach, where fishermen still ply their trade, is the larger; it is also known as the Cove or Fishing Beach. Swimmers favour the smaller Little Beach or Little Cove. Until the 1950s pilchard fishing was very important and in 1904 a record catch of 1,789,000 pilchards was landed over a four-day period.

Lizard Point Lighthouse The massed ships of the Spanish Armada were first sighted in 1588 from Lizard Point (above), the southernmost point in Britain. A lighthouse has warned passing ships of the Point's dangerous rocks since 1751. In the foreground are the slipway and the old lifeboat station; the lifeboat station was relocated to Kilcobben Cove on the opposite side of Lizard Point in 1961.

South Cornwall

Stretching from St Mawes Bay to Whitsand Bay close to the Devon border, south Cornwall has a beautiful gentle coastline dotted with attractive seaside towns such as Falmouth, St Mawes, St Austell, Polperro and Looe. Close to St Austell is the south-west's leading tourist attraction, the innovative Eden Project sited in a disused clay pit.

St Mawes The little town of St Mawes (above), at the end of the Roseland peninsula, is named after the Celtic saint Maudez. The sheltered harbour at the entrance of the river Percuil and good beaches nearby make this a popular destination with sailors and holidaymakers. There are ferry services across to St Anthony Head and to Falmouth. The surrounding coastline featured in the television series *Poldark* and Agatha Christie's classic *Murder Ahoy* was filmed in St Mawes. To the west of the town, St Mawes Castle was built at the same time as Pendennis Castle, and both are now in the care of English Heritage.

Maenporth and Pendennis Point Overlooking Falmouth Bay is the small town of Maenporth (above). Its gently shelving, sheltered beach is popular with families with young children. At low tide it is possible to see the wreck of the *Ben Asdale*, a freezer trawler that foundered in extreme weather on 30 December 1978 with the loss of three lives.

Pendennis Castle Fearing an attack by the French and Spanish because of his divorce from Catherine of Aragon, Pendennis Castle was built by Henry VIII in 1545. The castle escaped in that period because there was no invasion, but a century later it was besieged by Parliamentary forces during the English Civil War in 1646.

Falmouth When Sir Walter Raleigh visited Sir John Killigrew at Arwenack House in 1600, there was just a small hamlet where Falmouth stands today. Its geographical situation so impressed him that he advocated the site's development as a port. Falmouth harbour, along with the stretch of water called Carrick Roads, is the deepest natural harbour in western Europe and the third deepest in the world. Falmouth received its royal charter in 1661. From 1688, for more than 150 years, the town served as the Royal Mail packet station, through which every single piece of mail passed to and from Britain's burgeoning empire. News of Nelson's victory at Trafalgar, and of his death, was received through Falmouth's Fishstrand Quay in 1805. The arrival of the railway in 1863 brought further prosperity to Falmouth. Today's visitors come to enjoy the town's many gardens and sandy beaches, including Gyllyingvase Beach (foreground left). Falmouth docks (below) were developed from 1858 onwards. They now cover 74 acres with ship repair and dry dock facilities, fish landing and processing and oil storage facilities. Also on the waterfront is the National Maritime Museum Cornwall, a joint project created in 1992 between the National Maritime Museum Greenwich and the former Cornwall Maritime Museum. Toad, Ratty and Mole, the characters in Kenneth Grahame's book *The Wind in the Willows*, began life in a series of letters Kenneth Grahame wrote to his son in 1907 while staying in Falmouth's Greenbank Hotel.

St Austell Cornwall's largest town, St Austell was first mentioned in an account of a visit by Henry VIII. The town's prosperity was based on tin, copper and later china clay. Today visitors come to enjoy the beaches, the Eden Project and the Lost Gardens of Heligan nearby. The St Austell Viaduct (right), to the west of the town, carries the main London to Penzance railway line over the Trenance valley. It is 720ft (219m) long, 115ft (35m) high and dates from 1898. The building in the town centre (far right) is known as the Red Bank; it is now a branch of the NatWest bank. It was built by local architect Silvanus Trevail in 1898 using striking red bricks from Ruabon in north Wales.

Wheal Martyn North-west of St Austell lie the two 19th century china clay pits of Wheal Martyn and Gomm (right). Today this 26-acre site forms the China Clay Country Park where, in interactive displays, visitors can learn about Cornish china clay's long history since William Cookworthy first discovered it in 1746.

Eden Project Since opening in 2001, more than eight million people have visited the Eden Project (below), generating some £800m for the regional economy. The brainchild of Tim Smit, this environmental project is situated in a disused china clay pit three miles (5km) to the north-east of St Austell. During construction of this global garden some 800,000m³ of soil had to be repositioned on the site. Visitors can see coffee, bamboo and fruiting banana trees in the tropical Rainforest biome, which, at 3.9 acres in area, is the world's largest greenhouse. Grapes and olives thrive in the more temperate Mediterranean biome and in the outdoor biome lavender, tea, hemp and hops grow. The Core, an educational centre with classrooms and exhibition space, opened in 2005. In 2007 the British Construction Industry acclaimed the Eden Project as the best British building of the past 20 years. In recent years Eden's outdoor gardens have become established with magnificent displays in spring and summer for visitors to enjoy.

Fowey At the head of its estuary, the town of Fowey (right) has long flourished as a port. Overlooking its busy harbour and quaint cottages is Place House, a fortified manor house and home of the Treffry family since the 13th century. Opposite sits the parish church dedicated to St Finn Barr, the first Bishop of Cork. The church tower dates from 1460 and is the second highest in Cornwall. Every year in May, Fowey hosts the Daphne du Maurier festival of art and literature.

Polruan Enjoying a sheltered position away from the prevailing winds, at the entrance to the Fowey estuary, Polruan was once a busy shipbuilding port. The stretches of water known as Polruan Pool and nearby Pont Pill (below) are today favourite moorings for leisure craft. Polruan "castle" is a rectangular blockhouse (foreground left) dating from the end of the 14th century. This was linked by a chain to another blockhouse on the opposite bank of the estuary, and the chain could be raised to protect the harbour from the French or from pirates. The rocks to the seaward side of the Polruan blockhouse are known locally as the Washing Rocks.

A short distance upstream from Polruan is the attractive small village of Bodinnick. Right by the water's edge is Ferryside, the home of the du Maurier family since 1927. It was here in 1928-9 that the author Daphne du Maurier wrote her first book *The Loving Spirit*, first published in 1931. The house is today occupied by Daphne du Maurier's son and his family.

Sept 15   1978

To My Dear Phil —

on our 21st Wedding
Anniversary with my love
& all my thanks for the
many good things we have
enjoyed together since 1957,
not just naive art !

Yours

Tony.

Twentieth Century British

NAÏVE AND PRIMITIVE ARTISTS

SHEEP by James Lloyd

Twentieth Century British

NAÏVE AND
PRIMITIVE ARTISTS

Eric Lister
and
Sheldon Williams

Astragal Books . London

ACKNOWLEDGMENTS

The authors appreciate the invaluable help they have
been given by: Anthony Ashby (Crane Arts); Denis T.
Barker (Barkers of Lanercost); Cyril Caplan; Peter
Cochrane (Tooth Gallery); David A. Cross (Fine Art
Gallery, Bristol); Alex Gregory-Hood (Rowan Gallery);
Jill Hopkins; David Hurn (photographer); Anatole
Jakovsky; Andras Kalman (Crane Kalman Gallery);
Nancy Lloyd; Christine McGegan (The Gallery, Over
Haddon); George Murray; Mary Pearce; Michael
Servaes (New Art Centre, London); South London Art
Gallery; Sunderland Arts Centre; Bells of Cheshire;
Vincente Zammattio (Circle Gallery) and Bill Toomey
as well as all the artists who have been so co-operative.

First published in 1977 by Astragal Books
a division of The Architectural Press Ltd: London

ISBN: 0 85139 083 8

Designed by Graham Mitchener

FIRST COMMUNICANT AND THE FIERCE
BULL by Andrew Murray

CONTENTS

I N RECENT years artists, collectors and the general public have shown increasing interest in the variety, sensitivity and joy of naïve and primitive art. It is always difficult to attribute a cause to anything as complex as a shift in taste—economic, social and aesthetic factors all play a part—so perhaps it is more instructive to look at its origins; for one thing because they shed some light on the difficult distinction between the terms "naïve" and "primitive".

Serious interest begins at the turn of the century with the discovery of the great primitive works from Africa, Oceania and South America. Originally brought to light by ethnographers and archaeologists, it was not long before these artefacts came to the attention of the leading artists of the day—men like Picasso, Mondrian, Derain, Klee, Moore and Epstein. All of them, incidentally, were avid collectors and the influence on their work of the remarkable masks and wooden sculptures which found their way into their studios was immense. Thus it was through "recognised" artists that primitive art was introduced to the public. Because it paved the way to a new visual dimension—a new way of seeing— it meant that twentieth-century primitives like Alfred Wallis and James Dixon were viewed with eyes that only a century before might well have found their work to be at best crude curiosities.

The essence of primitive art is its uninhibited, non-intellectual quality—the rawness of the emotional response to the thing depicted. It was a quality that sophisticated admirers of primitive art could never capture, only assimilate.

This immediacy of response is what links primitive and naïve art. Not for nothing is naïve art sometimes called "art from the heart". But where primitive art transmutes an emotional response into an artefact, naïve art is an immediacy of vision, untrammelled by conventions, whether of education or accepted cultural values. The naïve artist paints what *he* sees, not necessarily "what is there".

Though primitive artists do not necessarily emerge only from primitive societies, on the whole naïve artists come from an environment that is more or less stable and developed. Outside Britain much naïve art is in fact peasant art, the work of those who were gifted craftsmen or who had other creative talents which were respected, encouraged (or even, in a modest way, patronised) by their fellows. Some of the artists were seers, with a direct and wonderful contact with the human, animal or natural world around them. Others—and they tend to be closer in feeling to the primitives—used art as a means of working out private obsessions and imaginings.

The destruction of the rural tradition in Britain, the first rural society to be swept away by industrialisation, means that peasant art as such is rarely found here, at any rate after the nineteenth century. British naïves an primitives have developed along their own lines, ofte as unrecognised loners, as the biographical notes in thi book show. But this, in a way, has also preserved then from the fate that has overtaken artists of this kind i other countries who have fêted them as national asset National assets are notoriously apt to be exploited an countries once famous for fine examples of peasan painting and carving have in too many cases spoilt th culture by ruthless exploitation. This is particularly tru of parts of Africa, and of Jugoslavia, Haiti, South Americ and Bali, in all of which countries tourism and culture ar ineluctably linked in a single ministry whose policy an business activities make the most of opportunitie afforded by "airport art". In this way the products local naïve and primitive art can quickly become debased commodity. Unfortunately there are many othe countries to a greater or less extent sharing in the sam fault (one thinks of the industry in "primitive" eskim carvings) with the result that true collectors in th sophisticated world's capitals no longer expect to discove real examples of primitive carvings from far away place except at prohibitive cost. The great naïve artists Jugoslavia, of Haiti, of Bali—men like Ivan Generali Rabuzin, Hyppolite and Ketig are no longer withi financial reach of any but museums or the richest collectors. The golden age of naïve and primitive art i countries of this kind has long since been passed. Touris who make their way along these well-trodden track will find little but second-rate trash to satisfy the longings for real local art, and it is a terrible irony tha so many of these prospective buyers are seduced by th exotic atmosphere in which they find themselve In such circumstances they come to believe that they hav actually *discovered something for themselves*. If the re works of art have disappeared or become too expensiv there are still substandard pieces. They will serve th purpose. Souvenirs of a happy holiday. Souvenirs, b simultaneously "art". The collapse of their good tas under a hot sun against a panorama of swaying palm would scarcely matter were it not for the disastrou effect it has upon the artists. Their standards take a div too. An easy market, pressures of demand and the chanc to pocket hard currency combine to adulterate the wor quality of all but the most incorruptible.

Many books have been produced in recent years abou naïve and primitive art in other countries, but none h been written about the British school. In part this ma be due to our national habit of not honouring ou prophets, but equally it may be attributable to th bewildering variety and complexity of the art that do exist and which the pictures in this book illustrat Shorn of a common cultural base, it would seem th British artists of this school feel free to express their ofte ighly individualistic whims and fancies. It may also explain why Britain is so rich in fantastic artists who, because they are compulsive in their painting and sculpture (and usually untrained) are also associated with the naïves and primitives.

Cultural and social environments, therefore, throw some light on the individuality of styles and themes that these artists display. But equally the way naïves and primitives set about the process of producing their work—from the heart, as we have said earlier—in itself produces the diversity. An illuminating analogy is that of jazz music, both in terms of performers, sometimes self-taught and unable to read music, and what they produce. Jazz musicians have the ability either to invent music straight from an inborn relationship to the instrument, or to select a tune, a melody, a twelve-bar blues and then improvise, perhaps letting the whole ensemble take off a jam session, with more and more immediate improvisation by soloists and the rhythm section (which the heart beat).

Is not this the same process through which the best naïve and primitive artists go? In each case the creative inspiration is automatic and immediate. Improvisation is as common to the one as to the other. Another parallel, too, extends with the performers. All kinds of people play and compose jazz; the same can be said about naïve and primitive artists—a true democracy whose common coinage is natural inspiration, vision and emotion.

When the layman thinks of jazz, he thinks of a certain type of sound, associated perhaps with someone like Louis Armstrong leading a band of musicians; but to carry the comparison further beyond its external characteristics even jazz, for the connoisseur, has its complexities. Just as there are many different types of naïves and primitives, so too jazz can be categorised under headings like New Orleans, Mainstream, Cool, Bebop, Swing or Avant-Garde.

It is more difficult to categorise primitive and naïve painting, for one thing because the distinctions between one style and another are seldom clearcut. Nevertheless people new to this kind of art and many visitors to galleries like the Portal Gallery, London, which specialises in it, are puzzled by its variety and complexity, as contrasted with their preconceptions, which are generally in the direction of something sweet, childlike, colourful and simple at one extreme or Lowry's stark industrial scenes at the other. They are apt to ask questions like: "Surely this isn't a primitive? It looks more like a Salvador Dalí". Indeed some lay readers of this book may find themselves wondering by what criterion certain artists have been included in it.

Categorisation in any field, and particularly in the arts, is a dangerous game, but to clarify the situation, we have attempted a classification of the various approaches to naïve and primitive art which the works shown in this book represent and to describe what these classifications mean.

Despite the fact that there is nowadays a growing interest in naïve and primitive art, the basic understanding between painters and collectors (or simply people who would like such a painting to hang on a wall) can still be rather rudimentary. Acclaim, when it comes, is often regional, indeed parochial. Museums have largely ignored it in this country (the Tate has only one picture by James Lloyd, probably one of the most remarkable twentieth-century British painters) and the same goes for critics. As for the media, they are more interested in gimmicks and eccentric personalities than in looking at this form of art in any serious way. So how do you tell good from bad? Like any kind of art there is good, bad and indifferent naïve and primitive art around. There are, of course, "big names" who are investments, if speculative ones. Or you can rely on the judgement of a dealer, who, over the years has acquired the knowledge and discrimination to pick out the genuine article from what is merely amateurish or, even worse, meretricious, and who is in regular contact with the painters. This is perhaps the best way for those who want to become serious collectors, for no established dealer wants to lead his clients astray. Or you can buy, at local exhibitions and galleries, what you yourself like. Naïve and primitive work is still inexpensive and there is no better reason for buying a work of art than simply the fact that you like it. It is certainly a point of view with which the artists in this book would be in sympathy.

Naives *Naive Art and Sentiment* Naive artists who betray in their work anything suggesting the soft and sentimental • *Naive Craft* Naive artists who have decided upon a specific craft with which to illustrate their vision • *Eccentric Naive* Naive artists who are offbeat in their choice of subject, their style, or in their eccentric imaginings • *Naive Humour* Using naive art as an instrument with which to poke fun • *Naive Innocence* A total lack of anything approaching visual sophistication • *Naive Mystics* Naive artists, and there are many, who have introduced mysticism into their works • *One-Track Naives* Naive artists who, in general, stick to one subject • *Naive Phantasists* Naive artists who inject elements of phantasy into their innocent vision • *Naive Realists* Artists of speckless reality which is still naive in origin • *Naive Sophisticates* Some of the artists who shelter under this contradiction in terms are occasionally referred to as faux-naives but nevertheless their work is not far removed from that of their more innocent colleagues • *Straight Naives* Direct naive vision. Less childlike than the works by the Innocent Naives, but in their way they are just as fresh and unsophisticated

Primitives The modern Primitive, rare and much to be treasured, differs from the primitive in less sophisticated parts of the world because he is divorced from an untainted primitive society

Phantasists The Phantasists combine a mixture of poetry and the product of a fertile imagination with the compulsive but generally untrained desire to create

Unplaceables The Unplaceables may share many of the attributes of the Naive, the Primitive and the Phantasists, but they have an indefinable independence of style and creativity which sets them apart.

CHOPPY SEA by Alfred Wallis

THE ARTISTS
AND THEIR WORK

2

Florence **ABBA** Derbyshire

ABBA (1920–1975) was born in Chorley, Lancashire. Dogged throughout her life by ill health, she did not start painting until after her husband's death in 1966. Unable to afford brushes, she painted with a needle, but not in the dot style of the late James Lloyd. However minutely performed, Abba's paintings gave the effect of a torrent of expressionist paint. Intensely religious in her own eccentric way, she sang hymns and recited prayers while working on her paintings. Her subjects were always drawn from inspired phantasies and their titles were just as extraordinary. When George Murray of Preston acquired *Sir Billy, a Star of Love*, Abba took a letter to Sir Billy and insisted upon Mrs Murray reading it to the picture.

Had it not been for her unconventional working methods and her delvings into a recognisably spirit world, Abba might well have been classed as a primitive. The painted framework around Sir Billy's portrait is not so far removed in its nature from the unsophisticated output of anonymous eighteenth and nineteenth-century sampler embroiderers. But that is where her simplicity ends; everything else about her paintings confirms that she was an artist of phantasy, fanatical in her determination to give her imaginative creatures visible form.

SIR BILLY, A STAR OF LOVE by ABBA, 1966

4

Elizabeth ALLEN

Elizabeth Allen (1883–1967) was born with a twisted spine and deformed leg in Tottenham, London. She was one of a family of seventeen children. She learnt to sew in the tailor shop of her German father while she was still a child. First in Suffolk, and later back in London, she earned her living as an independent sempstress, but when she finally moved to a little iron house in the woods near Biggin Hill, Kent she began work on her quilted and embroidered pictures. These, since the year before her death, have been seen in public in London (Crane Kalman Gallery), Los Angeles, New York and Germany.

However bizarre their subject matter, there is a kind of sublime passivity about Elizabeth Allen's little pictures. Her colours, often as rich as expensive Edwardian candies, somehow assert a sense of unabrasive order. The simplicity of her forms in no way deducts from the essential phantasy of characters like antique royalty, the angels and devils and prophets of the Old Testament, and a kind of never-never land of Mediterranean or Near East quietness and refinement.

It is this gentle charm which diffuses the nightmare in *The Dream of Nebuchadnezzar* in which the trouserless monarch crawls out of a cage watched by a horned figure looming in the background; and the same might be said of *The Population Explosion*. Mother, lying in the bed, betrays no alarm. The heads of the identical sextuplet family with her look more like those of cherubs than a matter of concern for the census.

Her dream and story embroideries suggest the innocence of childhood, not the sophistication of mysticism.

POPULATION EXPLOSION by Elizabeth Allen

John **ALLIN**

John Allin was born in Hackney, East London in 1942. He started his working life as a lorry driver who in his spare time took up painting trying to copy reproductions of Rembrandt pictures, but this proved unsatisfactory and he gave up painting until the mid-1960s when, with time on his hands, he began again, now not attempting to copy anyone.

His first "original" paintings were naïve in the most direct way. He made pictures of the world he knew (fast disappearing as more and more of East London became redeveloped), especially of local shops and characters. But since the days when he painted the policeman trying to dislodge a moody demonstrator from the top of a chimneypot out in some backstreet housing estate, Allin has gradually refined his technique. ("The policeman's uniform wasn't quite right," he says, "but I just felt I couldn't copy it from an official manual.")

The paintings of the Old Jewish East End that he made for the book *Say Goodbye, You may never see them again*, with pictures by Allin, and text by Arnold Wesker, show that he has become a much more *careful* painter, even if his naïve *vision* remains unimpaired.

His latest work will relate to the travelling circus, which he joined to acquire firsthand knowledge of the subject and with which he has already performed successfully as a clown in the professional arena.

He has been a regular exhibitor at the Portal Gallery in London since its directors first saw his pictures in the mid 1960s.

THE LIVE EEL MARKET by John Allin, 1973

Fred ARIS

Fred Aris was born in South-East London in 1934.

Besides his painting, his time is occupied with the café he inherited and with his interest in music (plainly evident in his brown and sepia study *The Three Musicians*). His pictures have the same free from dust "reality" to be found in the famous painting *American Gothic* by Grant Wood (1930). Aris is as neat, almost dapper, as his own pictures.

As well as his selections from the world around him, he has a penchant for the recent past and often chooses subjects which owe their inspiration to old postcards, faded photos and scraps from photo-illustrated magazines of times gone by.

There are certain archetypes which make their frequent appearance in the works of naïve artists (especially naïve realists), and one of these is *the cat*. Aris's painting of the nude kneeling on the chaise-longue gazing at her black cat is a superb example of this genre.

The naïve realists are a people apart from the other naïve artists, and certainly they have no kinship with primitive artists. Aris is one of the best of this type of painter even if occasional gusts of heavy humour or a warming sentimentality sometimes creep into his work.

GIRL WITH CAT by Fred Aris

Cliff ASTIN

Cliff Astin was born in Burnley in 1905. Since retiring from the coal mining industry, he has been a resident of Blackpool and, as a painter, is an avid recorder of its more massive, monumental and entertaining landmarks.

His pictures have the same brick by brick exactitude as those of the famous French naïve Louis Vivin, except that in Astin's case they have the gaiety (never stolid) of an iced cake instead of the Frenchman's cold masonry.

Whilst he has none of the speckless cleanliness of a naïve realist, in his straight naïve and innocent way Astin makes an edifice like the one in *Yates's Wine Lodge* live. A Riley car of the early 1930s that he once used for transporting a band and instruments can still be seen traipsing around Burnley today, a fitting subject for an Astin painting. Meanwhile, the sun shines brightly.

YATES'S, BLACKPOOL by Cliff Astin

Margaret BAIRD

Margaret Baird was born in Chirnside, Berwickshire in 1891. Today she lives in Preston. After leaving home, she took up dressmaking. She did not start painting until she was seventy-five years old, the year her husband died. Her first picture—a willow tree—was painted to amuse her grandson when he had measles.

Four years later she was awarded the prize at the Madrid Sport in Art exhibition.

This is a painter who likes to turn the local scene, especially if there are any games taking place, into direct innocent naïve paintings. When the art dealer and collector Andras Kalman bought one of her paintings at her first exhibition (in Manchester), he said "Mrs Baird's paintings are genuinely naïve and beautiful. They have a timeless appeal and are a bit of a respite in a world full of humbug".

CATTLE MARKET II by Margaret Baird

Harold Clarence BAITUP

H. C. Baitup was born in Heathfield, Sussex in 1904.

The country background for his painting, which he did not begin to do until 1939, was based on early experiences when his father was at work with horses at the Britannia Flour Mills, before switching to his own smallholding and subsequently becoming a fishmonger.

Harold Baitup had a lot to do with horses when he was a boy and later, with friends, he took great pleasure in the sports of the countryside, shooting, fishing and netting after dark. His rural life led him to try all sorts of employment—well digging, house decorating, plumbing, gardening and at one time even becoming a barber.

The early paintings, few and far between, were copied from illustrations in magazines, but when he retired he started to take his art life seriously, working first—for economy's sake—on rejected bits of wood and cardboard, and even replacing his brushes when they were finished with shaving brushes or a homemade brush of his own hair. Today he has been able to relinquish these outlandish props and use orthodox materials.

Baitup's intention is to communicate. Like Chesher before him, he is more concerned with accuracy than aesthetics. He is an innocent in his approach to the subjects he loves, but much of his untutored skill is of such a high order that he comes close to realism in his own personal way.

TIMBER HAULING by H. C. Baitup

Kenneth Dow BARKER

Kenneth Dow Barker, except for time with the RAF has always lived in Ingleton. Now in his sixties, he is completely familiar with the Lake District and the Yorkshire Dales. For many years he worked underground at Ingleton Colliery as a trammer with a dapple-grey pony until he left to tend the roads and hedges of the countryside he knew so well.

His first embroidery pictures (1955) were made after a visit to hospital when he was advised to abandon his active life. The actual embroidery craft was taught him by his wife Hannah, herself a skilled seamstress. He began by copying the pictures in children's books, tracing them on to linen for the amusement of his granddaughter, but today he is concerned with what he sees of country life, although occasionally he cuts out a picture from the local press if he thinks it would be a good subject for embroidery.

Kenneth Dow Barker's style and pictures are innocent, but his skill with the needle is that of an expert.

DISPLAYING THE SHEEP by Kenneth Dow Barker

Ralf BATES

Ralf Bates was born in Moss Side, Lancashire in 1931. "Shopless, publess hamlet in the Fylde" he calls it.

Bates has been in and out of countless different jobs, forrester, roof-tiler, poultry farmhand; he also served in Germany with the RMP and RAMC, worked in a workhouse hospital, painted crinoline ladies on mirrors for half a crown each. Then he took up serious painting under the patronage of Michael van Bloemen and Ben Pearl.

Some idea of Bates's frequent economic dilemma is illustrated by the action he took when he was at the centre of extreme financial difficulties and was able to set up a residence that would meet his requirements by creating a dug-out at the bottom of someone's garden. This kind of practical solution to life's problems is typical of Ralf Bates, an eccentric who was always prepared to take trouble to reduce immediate difficulties.

Subsequently he went on many travels, always carrying his painting materials with him; he hitched lifts, walked when there was no other alternative and got by with the minimum amount of cash, making his way through Europe, Iran, India, Ceylon and finally Australia where he took on a labouring job. During all this time he was able to keep up with his paintings of murals and posters.

Eventually, when he had managed to put together sufficient money on which to live, he went to live in a little bush shack where he could expand his painting, carving and writing activities in peace.

There were to be more adventures, hardships and eccentric events before he returned to England, with a further plethora of different jobs and varied employment. During the past twenty years of his life, his career pattern has been just the same, chopping and changing from one course to another. (He even worked at a teacher training college, and was once employed as a technician by the Tate Gallery.')

The above paragraphs say little about him as an artist, but they do indicate his complicated existence until now (he is currently gardening for what he calls "Rich Christians" and is writing a book).

Bates is an eccentric in his art output in the same way as he is in his lifestyle. He can make startling posters to advertise eccentric plays, or he can carve a child on a swing as a sign to hang up outside a restaurant. He once did a superb mural for a hotel in Spain which showed the tourists being devoured by a wild beast. An embarrassed management had it over-painted. Bates produces his own kind of utterly recognisable realism, but his naïve talent is as unpredictable as its standard is high.

WOODEN SCULPTURE by Ralf Bates

Gillian BECCLES

Gillian Beccles was born in England in 1918. Exactly where remains something of a mystery despite the authors' attempts to contact her for this information before the press date of this book.

For many years she has been a respected figure in the world of naïve art, both internationally and in Britain.

She is perhaps best known for her paintings of ships and the sea (although, as our picture shows, she is equally at home with other subjects). Her paintings are neat, direct and realist in a style much appreciated by the French, but she is not quite so exact as the naïve realists. A member of the Women's International Art Club, she has been represented in important international exhibitions of naïve art (Laienmaler at the Gewerbemuseum, Basel in 1961, Exposition Internationale de la peintre naïve at Circle Gallery, London in 1967, and Naïve Painting at Art Wagon Gallery, Scotsdale in 1972).

CARAVAN IN THE COUNTRY by Gillian Beccles

22

Frances G. BOND

Frances Bond was born in Newcastle-under-Lyme, Staffordshire in 1905, but she lived a number of years in China and Australia before returning to the North-West of England after the second world war. Today, she lives in Silverdale, Lancashire.

Her winsome kittens peering out of the bushes make good straight-forward claims upon the affections of petlovers. But she is a good deal better than that. Her sense of composition, however naïve, is taut and well devised. Her control of pigment and brush is professional.

Colours, however close to the lid of an old-fashioned chocolate box, are in keeping with her subjects. If the kittens are very white, grass and leaves and flowers are in bright contrast deftly applied.

DISCOVERED by Frances Bond, 1969

Helen **BRADLEY**

24

Helen Bradley was born in the Lancashire village of Lees in 1900. At first glance, her pictures look as if they had been painted solely for children. They have the right note of cosiness associated with successful, albeit sentimental, children's books. But since the publication of *And Miss Carter Wore Pink* in 1971, followed by *Miss Carter Came with Us* (1973) and now *In the Beginning Said Great Aunt Jane* (all from Jonathan Cape), there has been an extraordinary market reassessment of this naïve artist. Not only have the books been bestsellers, an ever-widening public has also been on the lookout for her pictures and—especially in the North—for signed reproductions of her works. She seems to have touched the rich vein of sentimentality not always so apparent amongst ordinary people.

She works in the quiet of her home in Wilmslow, Cheshire, far away from the bustling art world. The question of whether on the strict basis of quality her whimsy has a place in the long list of contemporary naïve and primitive artists of Britain is not going to be resolved by art critics or even art lovers (in the narrow sense); a much larger contingent drawn from the British public has decided that she is their *popular* choice.

GETTING READY by Helen Bradley

Caroline BULLOCK

Caroline Bullock, born in Cornwall in 1947, is just what every dealer in naïve art fears. She is the wife of a sophisticated and professional artist. They live in fashionable Islington. Her painting is therefore not subject to commercial pressures, she can paint when and how she likes and still not worry too much about the house bills. It is all the more to her credit that her pictures should have about them an unsullied innocence and simplicity that combine to make her a good naïve artist. Her colours are dry and very English, but the subjects of her paintings are sometimes imbued with the same kind of exoticism that crops up in the appliqué works of Elizabeth Allen.

IN THE BEER GARDEN by Caroline Bullock

Jean **BURTON**

Jean Burton, today in her forties and living in Surbiton, was born in England but at the age of six months was taken to the Argentine. During what she describes as a hectic life, she admits to having been married once, and sees herself as a painter who is also a poet-philosopher and the author of three plays.

The Tulip Field is typical of her work. It is a theme she has painted many times. She especially likes working on the same subject at different levels, at different times of day and at different seasons of the year. Her problem has been that she is not always true to her vision. Influences from a fashionable world outside have sometimes had a deleterious effect upon her work.

TULIPS by Jean Burton

"PATRICK" Byrne

Patrick Byrne was born in Glasgow in 1933, the son of a street busker. His family is important because of the strange course his art career was was subsequently to take.

As a young man he enrolled with Glasgow School of Art and in 1963 he was awarded a travelling scholarship to Italy. At Assisi he was deeply impressed by the primitive vigour of the paintings by Giotto, Cimabue and Duccio, all three of whom he reckons have left a permanent influence on his style as an artist.

On returning from Italy he took a job with a television studio as a *classical designer*. Then, after two years, he joined a cabinet factory, ostensibly to work on patterns for carpets.

In 1967 he painted what he considers to be his first "Patrick" picture, a small painting of a man in a panama hat holding some flowers, six by four and a half inches, painted in gouache on white card.

Until that time he had felt lost and unable to think of painting as a career, but a feature in the *Observer* colour magazine about naïve painters led him to believe that if they could work like that, so could he. The *Observer* had mentioned the Portal Gallery, so he sent the *Old Man in Panama Hat* picture to the Portal, but he also slipped a little note in the parcel to say that the painting had been done by seventy-two year old Mr Byrne.

The directors of the Portal were impressed but, like many other single paintings submitted by various artists, might this one turn out to be just a fluke? They wrote to seventy-two year old Mr Byrne asking him if he had any more pictures to show them. Within a month five more pictures arrived at the gallery. This time the response was even more positive. Would it be possible to arrange an exhibition of seventy-two year old Mr Byrne's work?

This letter when read by young Mr Byrne's wife was too much. She told her husband it was immoral to build up a false reputation for his father in this way. So in another letter the gallery was told the truth. The

Portal were quite happy to learn that their new artist was not a septua-
genarian.

Ironically, old Mr Byrne who had never painted a picture in his life
started painting shortly afterwards. "They're very naïve," says Patrick,
"the real thing, but the majority are not very good, Still, he's improving
. . .".

Today Patrick in a fulltime and quite prolific artist. Apart from sensa-
tionally successful exhibitions at the Portal, for the Third Eye Gallery
in Glasgow as recently as 1975 he spent ten and a half months completing
sixty paintings, several of them eight foot square in size.

Like nearly all the other artists in this book, he is an instinctive painter,
although in no other respect could he be called *naïve*. To modern eyes,
he is principally a painter who evokes the late Victorian era. This period
for him is a portrait of his grandparents' childhood (even though, with
wishful thinking, in the main he has made his children and people
comfortably middle-class). Below a certain age, the children in his
pictures—wearing long dresses covering layer upon layer of petticoats—
are sexless. They are like Victorian dolls of 100 years ago.

But his cumbersome children are frequently surrounded by a toy-world
of jack-in-a-boxes, hoops and tops, furry animals or roaring beasts
(miracles of taxidermy). Musical instruments are also often included in
the paintings, especially the banjo—plucked or strummed by black boys.
Even the Christy Minstrels are stirring.

Everything is still. Toys and the calves of children's legs have the same
sculptured rotundity. (Where are Giotto, Cimabue and Duccio?) Patrick's
colours are cool and careful. His paint is deftly applied. His pictures
strike a chord of enthusiasm in the hearts of his collectors and admirers.

CHILD AND LION by "Patrick" Byrne

Bernard CARTER

At one time a schoolteacher, Bernard Carter (born London, 1920) is today the Curator of the art section of the National Maritime Museum, Greenwich, a very suitable occupation for one who looks and dresses like a definitive British Civil Servant. But the museum at Greenwich is not only a natural niche for such a person on grounds of appearance, Carter is also absorbed with boats and waterways, especially what remains of the British canal system.

His paintings of these half-forgotten water links are in themselves valuable records of a bargee's map that can so soon become totally obsolete. Carter paints with the photo-realist intensity of a Dutch still life.

In fact his paintings have the same airless stillness that so often affects the compositions of the Dutch Old Masters. Even the ripples on his canals look as if they have been frozen into perpetuity. Perhaps they have.

THE BARGE by Bernard Carter, 1972

Jas CARTER

Nothing is known about this artist, whether he is alive or dead, where he was born, where he lived or if he had any other means of subsistence beyond his painting. His work therefore has to speak entirely for itself. It certainly has quality.

Painting on small wooden panels, this artist liked to colour large uncomplicated areas of landscape in browns and sepias and dark greens above whose horizon was a plain light blue sky. In the landscape itself would be two or three figures, different in size to establish the distance between them. These figures are drawn in ordinary pencil upon thinner pigment, partly to distinguish them from the rest of the painting but also so that the pencil lines could be seen clearly defined.

THREE ALONE by Jas Carter

Reg CARTWRIGHT

Reg Cartwright was born near Leicester in 1938. At one time his main interest was music. He was a trumpeter and when he was in the army, like the Douanier Rousseau, he played for the military. Since that time he has played trumpet in a local dance band and, more recently, has played with the university orchestra. For a while, he spent something like a third of his time designing sleeves for discs or making posters for concerts, but by 1969 he had become more involved in serious painting, and since 1972 has been a full-time artist.

Cartwright, the naïve realist painter is clearly visually (perhaps also socially) aware of the persons who make up the small community in which he lives and the parts its members play in making sure that this social structure works. He paints "portraits". Not portraits of personalities, but the essential and chemical make-up of recognisable local dignitaries and public servants, like the retired man in his garden, the postman, the town clerk or the local policeman.

If Fred Aris paints types (the dove-fancier, the personalities of the three musicians), Reg Cartwright paints local figures. Both artists employ the same unwavering clean finish throughout all they do.

THE PARK KEEPER by Reg Cartwright

38

"Barry" CASTLE (true name: Finbar)

Philip Castle's wife was born in Dublin in 1935. In their way her paintings are even more Celtic in style than those of her husband's. They have more the Irish flavour of the famous years before the twilight set in. Very different from Philip's sense of familiarity with the decorated interiors of Ravenna's domes.

In another more absurd age, Barry Castle might have worked upon escutcheons for the Royal College of Heralds or upon low-relief Stations of the Cross for well-furnished churches and cathedrals. Her pictures, whether they are culled from Zodiacal sources or from the lives of the saints are more in tune with the illustrations to the Minnesänger than with the gallo-romantic civilisation of the Roman South.

THE BALANCING ACT by "Barry" Castle

Philip CASTLE

Philip Castle was born in Southern England in 1929. His original ambition was to take up a career in nuclear physics, but this was eventually shelved with his practical realisation that however hard he worked upon the subject he was never likely to reach the top of the tree, and that there was too little room at the top anyway.

Looking at his careful and imaginative paintings today, it is difficult to realise that he was once a tempestuous artist whose pictures were closer to an expressionist primitivism than to the naïve. The change in his style (and intent) took place several years ago when he became fascinated by the religio-medieval legends of the Mediterranean (and the rest of Europe as well for that matter).

A painting by Philip Castle is a curious mixture, part second cousin to an illuminated manuscript, part mosaic of Near East complexity and brilliant hues; in one sense investigation into a sacerdotal phantasy and its practical application, in another a portrait of the weird world governed by nobles and their whims, both serious and comical. This strange melange in the hands of a competent and meticulous artist makes Philip Castle an attractive naïve sophisticate.

COUNT BELISARIUS PREPARES TO ATTACK A KILLER WHALE IN THE HELLISPONT by Philip Castle

A. W. CHESHER

Chesher spent all his life in Bedfordshire (1895–1972). A countryman, his whole existence was bound up with farming. But in his mid-forties he fell victim to two accidents, first losing the sight of an eye when a gun backfired and then catching his arm in a threshing machine. Tragic for Chesher, but quixotically fortunate for the art world.

Robbed of the opportunity to work on the farm, he turned to painting. But this was not yet another example of misfortune turning fosterfather to a new naïve talent. Chesher felt he had a specific job of work to do. His fascination with the steam traction engine, in all its practical forms, and what it could do to help agriculture led him to make paintings of the old machinery with a detailed fidelity unmatched in any museum because he painted them in all the bright and shiny colours they had possessed when they were first put to work. From the day he started until a year or two before his death (when he lost the impulse to paint any more), all his pictures were of his *beloved monsters*. The fact that even when he began they were fast becoming obsolete only spurred him to greater efforts.

He took all his deft seriousness of the study of the steam traction engine almost as a duty, basing it upon his own memories and what he had been able to learn about the machines from his father.

Glad though he was to play a significant part in the television feature Ken Russell made about the subject, he was more than a little displeased to discover that the congregation of so many of his favourites before the camera was for the purpose of conducting a race. These engines were not designed for racing he pointed out.

In his unique manner this artist found that he had two quite different groups of enthusiasts for whom he was working. Experts came to see his pictures because of the informative detail they could glean from them. (Chesher knew his subject. He never put a foot wrong.) Then there were the others who appreciated him solely for the eccentric one-track artist he was.

Sometimes he himself, either as a little boy or as a young man, would

appear in his paintings, and at other times friends or relatives, long since dead, were immortalised in this manner, but if the figures at work in his pictures had the same direct naïvety of the rural settings surrounding them, the same could not be said of the machines themselves. Their brilliant paint and metal work matched their accurate assembly.

In this category Chesher is unrivalled. His quiet way of life in the little house in a Bedfordshire village, even after he became a sorrowing widower, in no way reduced the off beat glamour of his wonderful paintings of vanished agricultural steam traction machinery.

JANUARY *1919* by A. W. Chesher, 1968

44

Beryl COOK

Beryl Cook was born in Reading in 1927, but she did not produce her first painting until one Christmas in Rhodesia (1964) when she painted a portrait of an Indian woman with huge breasts which the family nick-named "Hangover". It was done with a child's box of paints as a caprice and she did not paint any more until several years later when the family returned to Britain.

The Cooks started their new life in Cornwall. The walls of the house were bare and Beryl Cook started painting pictures to decorate the place. Not unlike Wallis and Dixon, the two great British primitive artists so different from Beryl Cook in other ways, she used discarded fragments of wood to paint upon, nailing them to the wall so that they would not warp.

The spirit of the Indian lady's portrait lived on. The new paintings were full of fun, often bawdy, but always snippets closely observed from the life around her. Today she runs a boarding house in Plymouth and her guests get a free show of her paintings: pub scenes, holiday girls on the beach, old people sitting in the promenade shelter (decorated with obscene grafitti).

The style she has evolved is rich with plump raucous humour (the sort sometimes evident in the paintings of William Roberts, Edward Burra and Stanley Spencer, but really going back to the uncensored hilarity of Thomas Rowlandson at his most mischievous). Take a look at her *Bowling Ladies* with one sticking her finger up the bottom of another stooping to take aim with the bowl.

With Beryl Cook, colours are always bright, flesh is upholstered and frequently rosy. Vulgar, perhaps; popular, certainly.

GOING BATHING by Beryl Cook, 1975

46

Gladys COOPER

Gladys Cooper (1899–1975) was born in Liverpool, but spent much of her life in Preston. She did not begin painting until she was fifty-two (the outcome of a lecture given by a Wigan artist and teacher. He told her to paint, but never to take a lesson).

She is described here as an Innocent Naïve because of the style of her work. In other respects, she was far from innocent. When she was not painting she divided her time between dispensing homoepathic medicines and casting horoscopes. All her paintings, no matter how simple in their make-up, are shot through and through with haunting echoes of what she called "our sinister times".

SOMETHING PENDING by Gladys Cooper

Ronnie COPAS

Ronnie Copas was born in Lambeth in 1936. Although he won a scholarship to an art school, family finances prevented him from taking advantage of it. But that did not stop him painting. He worked hard at his pictures from 1958 to 1965. Then followed a five-year break when he did not paint at all.

But in 1970, when he was working as a boatman for Lord St. Leven at St. Michael's Mount, he started again, this time using acrylics. Fascinated by local lore and history, his inspiration as an artist became completely transformed.

He became absorbed in a study of Old Master methods, particularly in tempera paint. The results were very strange. His new pictures had the look about them of some kind of Florentine transformation of the style of the late Sir Stanley Spencer. Completely self-taught, he managed in subdued hues to paint carefully composed pictures like the ones of the Nuns of Notre Dame de Syon setting out by boat for the Mount (once the Order's property, although never properly used for religious purposes), or of *After the Ground-Sea* (a natural but rare phenomenon on the Cornish coast when the sea, often from hundreds of miles away, throws up in the beach's sand all sorts of recognisable flotsam and jetsam from its depths).

Copas's work has extreme finish. His compositions are taut and well thought out. His subjects, like *The Channel Swimmer* (which he prefers to call *Lizzie at Sea*) are most unusual.

NUNS ABOARD THE VIKING HOBBLER by Ronnie Copas, 1976

Ralph CROSSELEY

Ralph Crossley was born in Crigglestone, Yorkshire in 1884. He came to Grimsargle near Preston in 1910 and lived there until his death in 1966. One of a family of ten children, he became a bricklayer by profession and was happily married until his wife died in 1936.

Crossley was eccentric in a number of ways. Despite the adequate wages he drew from bricklaying, he would still beg help from neighbours.

His paintings were often the direct outcome of stories he read in the press. If one of these appealed to him, he would cut it out, "do a picture" of it and glue the cutting on the back. But not all his pictures were like that, although their titles leave the viewer in little doubt about what they mean: *My Sister 1948—her soul has a fortnight's notice to find fresh tenancy*, or *The World's Fight for Civilisation Championship*. The latter shows a boxing match in which Hitler, with no caricature nonsense—he just happens to be a puny lowgrade pugilist with an absurd moustache—is knocked out by an athletic super-trim Churchill in a ring surrounded with gloating and recognisable faces.

His paint is spare and telling. His pictures tend to be small, but their content is vigorous and complicated. The message is pure and simple, but the natural ability far outstrips such innocence.

THE WORLD'S FIGHT FOR CIVILISATION CHAMPIONSHIP by Ralph Crossley

William R. DAFTER

William Dafter was born in London in 1901. At one time he was working in a munitions factory from which he was transferred to Blackburn during the second world war. He started painting after retirement, but he also finds time to make dresses for his wife and toys for his grand children.

Dafter's work teeters between the clean-edge realism of a naïve oleograph and the more vigorous treatment of paint in a picture like *Tears*, full of feeling and expression, remote from the rather icy, albeit richly coloured, *Mother and Child*.

THE TEARS by William Dafter, 1971

Alfred DANIELS

Alfred Daniels was born in London's East End in 1924. He still lives in London. He studied at the Royal College of Art, but he has been able to mould what he learnt into a personal style which, however close it comes to urban and landscape portraiture, retains an element of the brick by brick painting technique of the Frenchman Louis Vivin.

Daniels is far from naïve in his lifestyle which has led him to the authorship of several books, including one on the proper use of acrylic paints as a medium. He is currently much involved in preparing series of "portraits" of country houses in the Shires.

MAGDALEN BRIDGE, OXFORD by Alfred Daniels, 1973

Natalie d'ARBELOFF

It will be realised that naïves and primitives come in all shapes and forms. The mysterious Natalie d'Arbeloff once had an exhibition at the Travers Gallery (London 1972). From this it was evident that she had a primitive talent that expressed itself in fragments of wooden collage attached to her pictures. Each of these pieces of wood was decorated, usually with a simple image like a heart or a baby. Natalie d'Arbeloff is included in Studio Vista's book *Collage* (details of which are in the bibliography).

RAMONA by Natalie d'Arbeloff, 1966

Neil DAVENPORT

Neil Davenport was born in 1913. He started his working life as a photo-grapher, but the essence of his painting never had anything to do with the camera; instead it stretched back to his boyhood at Marlborough College where his father after a long and successful career in the Army had taken up the post of Bursar. As a schoolboy, Davenport's great enthusiasm was for luxury cars of the 1920s. He and his friends kept close track of these and on one occasion Davenport wrote to a dealer saying he would like to examine a splendid limousine. The car duly arrived at Marlborough College and the goodhumoured chauffeur took a teenage boy and his friends for a spin.

It was these vintage cars that sparked off his own version of naïve humour. He painted portraits of them, frequently playing the leading rôle in some elegant drama. But soon his canvases were still further embellished with astonishing scenes and characters from the Spas, the Grand Corniche, and even from Ruritania. Today these paintings are bought with enthusiasm in many parts of Europe (as well as Britain) where they enter collections of those who appreciate these glimpses of a world of Hapsburgs, Hohenzollerns, Bourbon-Parmas, Saxe-Coburg-Gothas and titles of all sorts, together with their magnificent estates and retinues.

Davenport paintings are neat. Colours are just on the rim of technicolor, but shorn of its brashness. The style is a simplistic realism, but the subjects inevitably suggest illustrations of a bygone era. The humour is wry.

LISTENING TO THE BAND by Neil Davenport 1969

John DEAKIN

John Deakin, who never saw his seventieth birthday, died sometime during the late 1960s. Like Davenport, although in every other respect different, he was for a while a photographer—a successful one at that. An exhibition of his *Paris photographs* was held at the David Archer Bookshop in Greek Street (once the haunt of poets like Louis MacNeice, David Gascoyne, George Barker, Ruthven Todd and Percy Wyndham Lewis). That was in 1936. At one time a friend of Francis Bacon, Deakin worked for a while with a Mayfair studio and even carried out photographic commissions for *Vogue* magazine.

At some point he gave up photography and turned to painting. The results from this change were remarkable. He painted with a kind of naïve purity rarely experienced in the works of any other artist. Apart from his glowing flower pictures and portraits of the pearly king and the pearly queen, he also liked to have a stab at painting the Royal Family.

Everything he did was rich and careful. The portraits had something about them akin to the great anonymous English and American naïve paintings of the eighteenth century.

Deakin drank too much. He died of drink. His luck as a painter had been abysmal, but there are still a few collectors like the van Bloemens who are proud to have works by him in their possession.

FLOWERS by John Deakin

62

Patricia DEHO

Patricia Deho was born in London in 1934. She spent her childhood in the Lancashire village of Coppull and attended school at a convent in Wigan. Today she is married and lives in South London working as a telephone operator.

This naïve artist has a clear control of acrylic paints and her brushes pick out detail nimbly. Figures, foliage, cars, and especially buildings are tightly drawn.

CALLING THE ANIMALS by Patricia Deho

Michael DEMPSEY

Michael Dempsey was born in Dagenham in 1944. He still lives close to his birthplace and has been in Essex all his life.

As a young man he switched from one job to another, but usually came back to plumbing work, the trade in which he had been trained.

From an early age he had always been interested in drawing, so it was a natural development for him to take to painting in his early twenties. He has natural skill of a high order and, although he has not yet had an exhibition of his pictures in an art gallery, some of his paintings have been chosen as illustrations for the covers of best-selling paperbacks.

Dempsey is fascinated by boats and likes to make paintings of them. His favourites are the old sailing ships. Other subjects personally dear to him are the flat landscapes of East Anglia against which he likes to pose large-scale figures.

His kind of painting belongs in the same bracket as that of Fred Aris and Reg Cartwright. He is another naïve artist of careful realism.

THE AIR-RAID WARDEN by Michael Dempsey

James DIXON

James Dixon was born on Tory Island off the coast of Ireland in 1887. His death, in the early 1970s, took place not far from the exact place where he lived all his life.

Dixon and Alfred Wallis can claim to be the two greatest primitive artists Britain has ever known. Just as Wallis was *discovered* by the artists Ben Nicholson and Christopher Wood, so Dixon too was *discovered* by an artist—Derek Hill. But unlike Wallis who was at least made aware of world respect in his old age, no such fame was to be Dixon's during his lifetime.

Wallis had done his bit of travelling before settling down permanently in St. Ives, but Dixon never left stormgirt Tory Island.

Not surprisingly, most of his pictures relate to his island home—gales at sea, coastal scenes (some of them painted as if from the sky)—but occasionally when something epoch-shaking took place like the appearance of the R100 airship in the sky, Dixon would record that in a painting too. Like Crosseley (and perhaps with more excuse, because his paintings are rough, primitive and fierce instead of carefully informative), he wrote generally crudely inscribed and often misspelt titles and explanations of his paintings on the pictures; but unlike Crossley, Dixon wrote his messages on the picture's front.

The turbulent paintings by this artist show a clear primitive understanding of the hard life cut off from the mainland. Sea and sky and land are sometimes all fused together in a gigantic conflict. The paint, mostly close to a monochrome admixture of dirty blues, greens and greys, is slapped on with a passion that creates an almost abstract effect.

MULDOON CAUGHT IN A RING NET by James Dixon

Tom **DODSON**

Tom Dodson is one of the artists outside London (so often from the North) who becomes taken up by an agent-dealer with faith in the painter as a potential financial success. This manner of art marketing has become increasingly active north of the Wash, especially in the promotion of naïve or near-naïve artists. The "prints" (signed reproductions actually) by Lowry, Helen Bradley and Joe Scarborough are outstanding examples of this kind of popular trading, and in Dodson's case his prints are being mail-order sold by the Cheshire company Bells.

Dodson himself is an artist of the townscape. His pictures have the same accent as those of John Allin, but they are slightly cruder in intensity than the Londoner's and he does not have the same talent when it comes to painting people, although he does have a natural gift for catching figures in movement. His houses and streets are dour.

SNOW SCENE by Tom Dodson

C. Hamilton ELLIS

Hamilton Ellis was born in 1909 at Weston, but he received the most important share of his education in Munich.

What Chesher sought to do for the agricultural steam traction engine, Hamilton Ellis has achieved for the steam-powered railway locomotive, although his approach to this task could hardly have been more different than that of the Bedfordshire farmer.

Initially a writer upon the subject of the "Age of Steam" (he is author of some thirty books about locos), he had always enjoyed painting and making drawings of the big trains. The change in his life pattern came about when he finally became incensed by the low quality of illustrations submitted for his books by outside artists. It occurred to him that he could do very much more satisfactory work himself. More or less, until that time, painting for him had been an "extra".

This does not of course mean that he has entirely abandoned writing, rather that increasingly more time has been spent by him upon painting.

Like Chesher, he also makes the human element in his pictures subsidiary (although he takes care that the costumes of any figures are in keeping with the time when the train was in service), but unlike Chesher he scarcely qualifies for the description naïve, except that he too is clearly a compulsive painter and is a self-taught artist.

If Chesher's steam traction engines are essentially local and English, Hamilton Ellis's locomotives belong to all parts of the world. They too are painstakingly accurate in detail.

CASTLE HOWARD YORKS SCARBOROUGH LEEDS EXPRESS *1901* by Hamilton Ellis

72

Donald **FOX**

Donald Fox was born in London in 1919. To say that his subjects derive from physics and zoology is an oversimplification. He first came to the notice of the art world when the respectable "post-impressionist" British artist Claud Rogers (who made his reputation in the 1920s and later spent ten years teaching at the Slade School of Art) showed his fantastic paintings to the Portal Gallery.

Fox suffered experiences during the war which he will not discuss. They, along with other factors, probably explain why today he is almost a recluse. He is an artist, withdrawn in character, who spends most of his time at home.

A man of considerable culture, he occupies many hours with painting esoteric pictures which flow from the innermost recesses of his imagination. In their way some of these pictures recall certain types of work by Paul Klee. Curious animals and vegetation, along with abstract creature-like figures, appear in bright blobs of colour—orange and purple splotches, painted in watercolour on random sheets of paper. In his way, he is like an artist producing evidence of scenes which could be throwbacks to an earlier civilisation of which man has no record.

THE ARRIVAL by Donald Fox

74

Richard GARDHAM

Richard Gardham, the Yorkshireman is now in his forties. In his way he is also something of a mystic, although this does not come out in his work. Nothing of his interest in esoteric and philosophical cults can be seen in his portraits. Very suitably, as an itinerant gardener, he loves nature.

Of all the artists in this book he is perhaps the most *English*. In another social setting, in another time, he might easily have been a member of the Euston Road School. The colours of his pictures are the acme of moderation. He paints portraits—but of whom? Maybe the people in the pub (as in his picture of a man's face seen through the bottom of a pint beer mug), although he does not get anyone to pose for him. And style? Self-taught Gardham exhibits considerable mastery of a loosely-knit control of pigment. *Old Man* has just the requisite fuzz. The image is blurred, but the portrait of old age is immediate. Only the eyes are alive in a face that has already given up. Furry face, furry collar and furry cap all blend together. Only the hard outline of the dark coat makes sure that this is reality instead of here today gone tomorrow memory.

OLD MAN by Richard Gardham

Madge GILL

Madge Gill (1884–1961) was born in London's East End. This artist was a weaver of consummate skill, and something of this ability spilled over into her odd pictures (all of them tied up with a spirit world of which she claimed to have firsthand knowledge). These strange compositions were carried out principally in indian ink, sometimes on a scale extending twenty-six feet in length. Inspiration for these works was all supposed to stem from her spirit guide *Myrinnerist*, but it is a factor not to be overlooked that nearly all the "faces" in her pictures have a generic oval form suggesting a self-portrait from long ago.

Madge Gill spent the last forty years of her life hard at work upon pictures, but it is easy to see that something of the complexity of these designs is carried over directly from her years of experience as a talented creator of silken mats. This artist had a strong following and clientèle in spiritualist society, conscious that, at last, it had discovered a genuine talent firmly associated with their beliefs.

MYRINNERIST by Madge Gill

Dale GOFFE

Dale Goffe was born in Malta in 1931, but he was educated in England before joining the Merchant Navy as a boy, a career that ended when he lost an eye at the age of twenty-three. Despite this handicap, to earn a living he was able to master the art of photography. His camera took him to many parts, and it was while he was roving Scandinavia and the Mediterranean building up a series of suitable illustrations for picture magazines that he became interested in painting, a new enthusiasm which soon became his overriding concern in life.

From 1961 he spent all his time painting pictures. These were mainly of ships and he had a special delight in recording the obsolete—old paddle-steamers and craft that had long since been abandoned.

Completely devoid of any art training, he was able to paint exact portraits of ships with a fluency that made his work attractive to sailors and men on land alike. His accuracy and fluke ability made him a welcome contributor to exhibitions sponsored by the Royal Society of Marine Artists.

PADDLE STEAMER IN A CHOPPY SEA by Dale Goffe

Arthur GOULDING

Arthur Goulding was born in Bradford in 1921 and now lives in Black-pool. In his youth he toured the halls (including London's Windmill Theatre) with a musical group made up from his own family. Since 1965 he has divided his time between painting and his career as a professional musician.

He has a string of exhibitions in the North behind him, and his work has also been seen in Paris, Lugano and London (Grosvenor Gallery) and the Royal Society of British Artists.

Goulding paints with a kind of tight neatness much appreciated by enthusiasts for naïve art in France. Nevertheless, his choice and handling of subjects is very British. In *The Family*, those who look sharply can see that there are more than the three main characters in the picture. This is theatre stuff. The make-up mirror framed with light bulbs re-flects not only father in a shimmering stage costume, his wife with the naked baby on her lap, but also some ghostly figures in the background.

Perspective is careful, almost academically so, but not the treatment of figures whose innocent naïve-style appearance gives his works their subtle difference.

THE FAMILY by Arthur Goulding

Anne GRAHAM

Anne Graham was born in Vienna in 1925. She studied (although scarcely in the academic sense) with Professor Czizek at the Austrian School for Talented Children.

Her paintings have been exhibited in Naples and Australia (six times) and in Britain (Petit Gallery 1972), and her work has also been seen in group shows like those of the Essentialists and the Contemporary Art Society.

She possesses a keen understanding of paint and the many ends to which it can be put. Although she lays on the pigment in a smooth and careful manner, a considerable number of her pictures come as an unusual surprise to viewers because of their irregular shapes. Like Anthony Green, she believes that the orthodox choice of rectangle, oval or circle is not sufficient. Green, however special, can be put into one or another category of naïve painting. With Anne Graham, this is not so easy. Her style is straight naïve, almost realist, and her colours range from cool nuances to hints of tropical experience, but the quaint unreliability of the shapes of her pictures unquestionably sets her apart. This visual paradox is as much at variance with ordinary experience as a collage by Rembrandt would be.

THE OUTING by Anne Graham

Anthony GREEN

Anthony Green was born in London in 1939. In no sense can he be regarded as self-taught despite the very personal appearance of his paintings ever since they were first shown in the Young Contemporaries Exhibition of 1956. In the succeeding twenty years he has had nineteen one-man shows (eight of them in London's Rowan Gallery and the rest scattered round the world—New York, Stuttgart, Haarlem, Rotterdam, Helsingborg, Malmö, Hanover and Tokyo); he has also been represented in forty-nine mixed exhibitions and has been the recipient of four major awards including the Harkness Foundation, USA (1967).

Green studied at the Slade School of Art and four years later became a teacher there. He lived in Paris for two years and is familiar with the United States (through Harkness). His works can be found in sixteen public collections. The list of his achievements and degrees of his official recognition seem endless.

Yet, however sophisticated, his paintings—starting with the murky white-and-brown-and-clay-coloured Hogarthian portraits he made of his family a quarter of a century ago—have always been redolent of a kind of straight naïve vision.

At the beginning of his career as a painter, and for many years after, he settled for a direct chronicle of his family, especially the history of his courtship, marriage and fatherhood. But inevitably the circle widened to take in friends, associates and even casual acquaintanceships. What did not deviate was his conviction that all these characters should be painted in his own way, even if the rougher style of 1962 was fined down over the ensuing years. During that period the perspective in his paintings has developed a crazy geometry of vistas, frequently (as has been noted in the case of Anne Graham), pointed up by the extraordinary variations he has made from the irregular shapes of some of his pictures.

In still other ways, Green has changed. Raw youth is being replaced by gentler approach gleaned from experience. Romantic garden flowers find their way into vases in good taste set upon heavy tablecloths.

RED CRUCIFIX by Anthony Green

Vincent **HADDLESEY**

Vincent Haddlesey was born in 1934. Before turning to painting, he was a horse wrangler and rodeo rider in Canada, the United States and Mexico. At one stage he also trained racing and hunting horses in Britain. As an artist he has exhibited in Paris, New York and Canada. Works by him have also been seen at the Arthur Tooth Gallery in London. He lives in Paris.

The Haddlesey horse tends to crook his foreleg, a sophistication that shows he has firsthand experience of horses, after that everything about his work is straight naïve. If people in his paintings have expressions, at least they do not stretch into caricature (as they can in some Italian naïve paintings). The problem about his pictures is that they are just too flawless. There ought to be a fly in every ointment. There are none in Haddlesey's.

GYPSY CARAVAN by Vincent Haddlesey

Fergus HALL

Fergus Hall was born in Scotland in 1947. He and Caroline Bullock rank as the youngest artists under consideration in this book. Although he had received some art training, it must be made clear that "Feegie", as he is known to his friends, set aside all this experience when he got down to the serious business of producing his own paintings. At first this was a secret occupation. The pictures were of his own imagination; they were like scenes from some magical play (his father had been a theatrical scene painter, and Fergus Hall had always found the make-believe side of theatre fascinating), but this private side of his life suddenly became public when his fellow Scot, the artist "Patrick" Byrne persuaded him to take paintings down to London to show the Portal Gallery.

Within a very short period of time he became one of the gallery's artists and was commissioned to paint entire exhibitions of his work for showing there. The public proved no less appreciative of his naïve phantasy paintings and he even found his way into the music world—Feegie is an accomplished guitarist—designing record sleeves for King Crimson group and, on one felicitous occasion, he was commissioned to make the deck of Tarot cards for the James Bond film *Live and Let Die* after the original designs by Salvador Dalí had been turned down by the production office.

His pictures, forthright magic, indicate nothing of the natural shyness of this Scotsman. He paints worlds that blend phenomena with medieval sorcery, flecks of science fiction and the uncanny: persons, creatures (few of them recognisable), figures in landscapes and places that can only lurk in the mind of someone sensitive to the most outlandish fairytale or a world of sheer phantasy.

The paint is laid on smoothly with an almost eggshell finish. Everything is clear and at home in an existence of near-classical perspective. Only the subjects of the paintings themselves are mysterious.

The fisherman's inflated arms and his tiny hands underline practical concern for the job in hand. There could be a big fish in the painting

Owl by the River by Bernard Carter

Hay by A. W. Chesher

LISTENING TO THE BAND by Neil Davenport, 1969

One Bowling Lady Giving Another Bowling Lady a Surprise by Beryl Cook

King Nebuchadnezzar and the Demon by Elizabeth Allen

Workers' Cafe by John Allin, 1974

PIGEON FANCIER by Fred Aris

JOJO AND HIS BANJO by "Patrick" Byrne

THE GARDEN by Reg Cartwright

A Hat Too Big by James Lloyd, 1972

FIGURES IN DECK CHAIRS by Toby Lyon

THE PLOUGHMAN by Andrew Murray

Joseph Grimaldi Butterfly Hunting by Patricia Neville

St Michael's Mount by Bryan Pearce, 1972

Untitled by "Patrick" Byrne

THE CLOCKWORK BIRD by Anthony Green, 1974

ABOVE HOOD BRIDGE by Hamilton Ellis, 1969

Noah's Ark I by Fergus Hall

Boy and Horse by James Lloyd

Fishing in the Magic Pool. Hauling them in might be difficult for the angler perched on the swingseat he has hanging from the branch of a tree. The woodland behind is dark and dense—only the magic pool and the fisherman are in full daylight. This painting is typical of Fergus Hall's personal phantasy, but he can bring the same wealth of invention to a universal subject like *Noah's Ark* perched on the tip of Ararat while Mrs Noah, bar of blue soap in hand, takes a dip.

FISHING IN THE MAGIC POOL by Fergus Hall

90

Gertrude **HALSBAND**

Gertrude Halsband was born in Mossley (near Ashton-under-Lyne) in 1917. By profession, she was a dress-designer. After a year in London, and just one year before the end of the war, she married her husband who is a tailor, and the two of them were lucky enough to find cheap accommodation just behind Harrods (a happy circumstance which later led to her creating one of her most notable works, a naïve painting of the Tea Room at Harrods).

Tea also features in 'Come to Tea'. Someone comes in with a special cake. This is Harrods-land, so she wears an apron. The three girls at table are svelte, the chairs are pseudo-chippendale, an over-stuffed easy chair is close to the china cabinet on whose top the lumpy clock stands with its hands at half-past three.

Gertrude Halsband paints a London she knows and loves. She is an accomplished naïve, able, like many of her kind, to reconstruct the ordinary world in a fashion that gives it extra edge.

COME FOR TEA by Gertrude Halsband 1976

92

Harry **HARMER**

Harry Harmer was born in the Borough, South-East London in 1927 and he has lived in that area ever since. His regular employment has been as a gardener for Lambeth Borough Council, and he is still active in that rôle.

Harmer's innocence as a naïve artist is not only present in the imagery of his pictures, he also uses very "innocent" materials—pencil with water-colour-tinting on paper. On first impact his paintings could so easily be the product of the art room of a school, but what distinguishes him from infant prodigies is his true sense of place and people. Despite or perhaps because of the sparseness of his materials and instant naïvety of vision, he is able to imply the same day-to-day monotony of games in the street, the trudge back home after a working day, or even the *rarity* of a day on the beach at the seaside. The beach aside, he is a presenter of the eternal sameness of backstreets and council houses. It must have been the unfamiliar drabness of his London that made his 1971 exhibition at Studio Margutta 13 in Venice such a success.

NEAR KENNINGTON by Harry Harmer, 1964

Patrick HAYMAN

Patrick Hayman was born in London in 1915, but he lived in New Zealand from 1936 to 1947 (during which time he attended art school). He started painting seriously in Dunedin in 1938.

He was the founder-editor of *The Painter and Sculptor*, a magazine which ran from 1958 to 1963. He has exhibited in many galleries (mostly in Britain, but he also had an exhibition in Mexico). Besides being a painter, Patrick Hayman is also a poet. He operates on two levels, with brush and with pen. Sometimes he combines the two, including his verse in his pictures. A cultured man, he can scarcely be mistaken for an innocent naïve, yet his best work has an uncomplicated purity.

He paints in a dry vivid fashion, and he is not indifferent to the temptations of collage. Most of his works are on a small scale. The messages imparted by his paintings are ruthlessly direct. His warships are at war. Knights in armour are ready for mortal combat. Tristan loves Isolde. If he has to meet the twentieth century, he does so head-on with a self-portrait of himself as a flying machine.

SELF-PORTRAIT AS A FLYING MACHINE by Patrick Hayman

Peter HEARD

Peter Heard was born in London in 1939. Despite the high finish of his naïve realism, he is completely self-taught. By profession he is a civil engineer and bridge builder. He has been painting since 1970.

His pictures, generally on the small side, frequently feature personalised men or women carefully dressed and sporting the correct headgear. There is one character who is usually fully moustachioed and bearded. In style, neatness, and colour his paintings look as if they belong in the same bracket as those of Reg Cartwright or, in so far as style and speckless imagery are concerned, he could be said to have something to do with the methods of Fred Aris (but lacking the addition of Aris's chubby humour or occasional lugubrious character).

THE GARDENER by Peter Heard

Peter Heard.

Perle HESSING

Perle Hessing was born more than sixty-five years ago in Zaleszcyzyki, at that time a provincial township in Austria. As a child in Cernowicz she was strongly influenced by her father, a printer and bookbinder, who filled her mind with a detailed and complex knowledge of the Jewish mysticism and legend as revealed in the Bible and the Talmud.

Both she and her husband fell victims to the Nazi persecution during the second world war but, after peace was declared, they managed to emigrate to Australia and it was here, following a visit to London in 1962, that she was suddenly seized with the urge to paint.

And it was from the beliefs and stories instilled into her by her father so many years ago that this impulse drew its inspirations.

Perle Hessing paints like an illustrator, often employing the narrative style of the middle ages (in which the prime characters appear more than once in the picture as the plot unfolds). What she has to tell may not always be familiar to those seeing her pictures, but the manner in which she paints presents no visual problems. Imagery is naïve and easy to interpret or recognise. The colours are the bright or mysterious hues of fairy tales or exotic picture books. The paints themselves are laid on with only one intention, to colour the picture, and their application is flat and tints tend to be primary and glowing.

Working slowly, Perle Hessing produces pictures which are a feast for the eye. Typical of her strange gift is the manner in which she is capable of putting it to work. It is one matter for her to paint a number of versions of the awe-inspiring "Golem" of Prague, but she has shewn herself equally adept at undertaking an astonishing "life-story" picture of the philosopher Spinoza (all the focal points of his life, plus his ambitions, and even his dreams). This compendious picture (in full colour) is being reproduced as the frontispiece of her husband Siegfried's book *Speculum Spinozanum* which has been compiled to celebrate the new Spinoza centenary of 1977 internationally.

Since 1972, she and her husband have lived in London.

HOMAGE TO SPINOZA by Perle Hessing

Betty HOLMAN

Betty Holman was born in Camborne in 1911. Although she has spent most of her life in Cornwall, between 1958 and 1967 she lived in Ibiza. It was on that Spanish island after the first four years that she started painting.

Although she is the mother-in-law of the sophisticated modern painter Douglas Portway, no suggestion of the kind of background this relationship might have provided appears in any of her work. From the start, the style and nature of her painting have been without qualification naïve. Work like the *Fishmarket* with its haphazard perspective, its carefully prepared flat personages (together with miniature dog and half a cat) and the neat arrangement of the fish on the stall show her to have an innocence unaffected by the fifty-one years she lived before she painted her first picture.

On Ibiza, Ivan Spence the recognised promoter of all kinds of good artists immediately offered her a show and this first exhibition proved an immense success. Since that time her pictures have been seen in London at the Drian and Marjorie Parr galleries, as well as in Europe. Today she lives in St. Ives.

ST IVES IN NOVEMBER by Betty Holman, 1963

Dora HOLZHANDLER

Dora Holzhandler was born in Paris in 1928 of Russian-Jewish parents. She came to England at the age of six and subsequently attended the St. Martin's School of Art in 1943 (she later took part in the activities of the Anglo-French Art Centre at St. John's Wood), returning to France in 1945 when she studied at La Grande Chaumière and the Atelier St. Jacques. She returned to Britain about twenty years ago and has resided here ever since.

Dora Holzhandler, who had turned her hand to many occupations, including art modelling, utterly rejected her basic training in art schools, resorting instead to a very personalised form of naïve expression. Working in a style that looks like a fusion between that of the West and the Near East, she has set about making paintings of the world about her: subjects like a nude in a bath, a girl on a swing, a flower shop, or lovers transformed into rich colours (often made more intense in the contrast afforded by the introduction of a black and white mosaic tiled floor).

The faces of her figures are smooth and oval. The impression they give is one of happy peace (possibly because Dora Holzhandler herself is an enthusiastic believer in many of the lessons taught by Eastern mysticism). Hers is a strange variation in the rich treasury of naïve art.

THE BATH by Dora Holzhandler, 1964

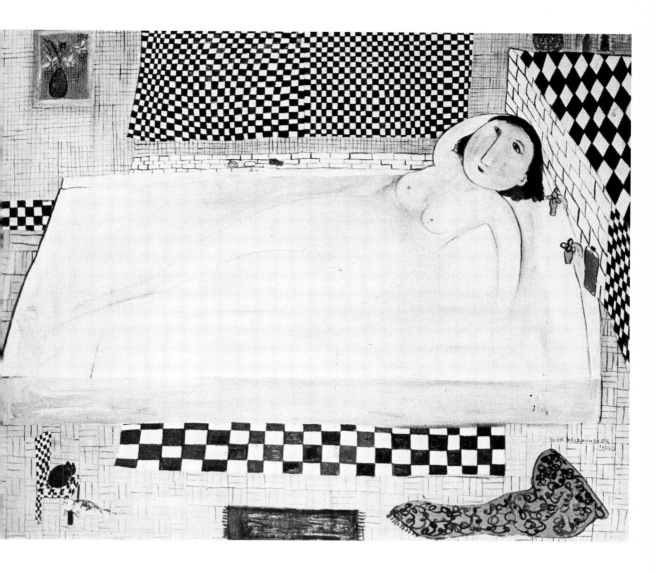

Elizabeth HOPKIN

Elizabeth Hopkin, now in her late fifties, was born in the upper Swansea valley, Wales. Her father had been a photographer, and her husband is an architect, so perhaps it is curious to find that with this professional background, when she took up painting a few years ago (originally to please children) the nature of her watercolour pictures was that of an innocent naïve, even if she fell between the two stools of seeking to record her memories of a Wales that has vanished and the pleasure of what she has come to regard as an enthralling pastime. Her first exhibition at the Portal Gallery in 1976 was a big success.

THE TRIP by Elizabeth Hopkin

John JACKSON

John Jackson was born in Radlett, Nottinghamshire in 1930. By trade he is a steelwelder at the Rolls Royce plant. His skill in this field is recognised and when in 1967 he gave up his pastime of boxing (largely because of a hearing defect), he took pleasure in what he describes as *doodling* with the welded steel offcuts. At first he attempted to make figures of boxers out of this raw material, but subsequently he tried to fashion pieces associated with horticulture (because his father is a prize-winning gardener. Some of the trophies awarded to Mr Jackson Senior were actually designed and carried out by his son).

It was by this time that he felt that he had conquered the working and creative problems of this intractable medium. Rolls Royce admired what he was doing and gave him considerable scope to do more.

Professional opinions about his work vary. Some certainly find his figures illustrating the tales of Robin Hood (it must be remembered that Jackson is a Nottinghamshire man) too sentimental, too close to kitsch. Nevertheless his ability goes unquestioned. He has taught himself a most unusual skill.

THE SWING by John Jackson

Gwyneth JOHNSTONE

Gwyneth Johnstone is reticent about her age, reticent too about her family background, but nevertheless the fact cannot be disguised that she grew up in a milieu of artists and, not surprisingly, served her own apprenticeship at the Slade School of Art.

Despite the individuality of her work, there is more than a smattering of impressionism in some of the effects she evokes, and it is this which lends her paintings a paradoxical sophistication.

The people in her pictures have a strong lyrical character, so too do the landscapes, the woods and cottages. The painting *Fishing Boats* also has the same touch of poetry about it. In its way it comes close to the Breton paintings of Christopher Wood.

It is difficult to show in reproduction the nuances she is able to introduce into her paintwork, the gentle swell of the sea, the boats looking like tubs, and the naïve trees that appear to have been cut out of cloth or leather.

Much of her subject matter is drawn from the remoter corners of France and Spain, and especially from the Norfolk that she knows so well.

Something of her nature, her poetic vision and how these are fitted into ordinary life is indicated by the story about one of her exhibitions at the Portal Gallery in the mid-1960s. As has been the case with several artists, at the opening of her show she had misgivings about one of the pictures. To put the matter right, she asked the directors if she might borrow the keys and let herself in after closing time so that she could make a few alterations.

The next day all was not the same. The goat prominently posed in front of a house in a French village had disappeared. Only the blank road remained. It was as if the creature had wandered off into the night.

The trouble was that this painting had already been sold.

A telephone call to Gwyneth Johnstone brought a forthright explanation: "Oh well, I didn't really like the goat, so I painted it out. Don't you like it better now?"

"That's not the point. What are we going to say to our client?"

There was no answer to the second question, but when the buyer came to collect his picture he did not even notice that the goat was missing, and when the gallery's directors mumbled something about the artist deciding to effect some alterations before he picked it up, he seemed quite delighted that she had paid him this "special attention".

FISHING BOATS by Gwyneth Johnstone

Joseph KEARSLEY

Joseph Kearsley was born in Leigh, Lancashire in 1908. He earned his livelihood first as a miner and then as a steel worker. He has been painting since 1950. He now lives in Tyldesley close to his birthplace.

His concern is not with pictures or painting, but with likenesses. It is the entirely primitive nature of these likenesses which sets him apart from the naïves. They see themselves as artists in whatever broad sense of the term they like to interpret the word, while Kearsley's ambition is to paint a collection of portraits of everybody who *matters*.

Prince Charles gives a visual idea of how this primitive inner compulsion to paint portraits of the great works out. Kearsley paints the young prince with almost caricaturist's understanding of what features to emphasise. The paint is coarse and flat, almost toneless. Kearsley is a natural. He is no Sargent, nor has he any intention to be so.

PRINCE CHARLES by Joseph Kearsley

April KERR

April Kerr was born in Leigh Woods, Bristol in 1921. She has only been painting pictures since 1972 (and since 1975 she has also been sculpting animals). Before that time she was fully occupied living the life of a grande bourgeoise in comfortable homes, scarcely interrupted by boarding school and finishing school in Paris followed by two marriages, first to Comte Maurice Retout du Trevou (two children) and then to Major Colin Kerr-Peterson (two more children). Today she lives in Somerset.

As a teenager, she remembers a visit to a country house when a footman in full livery (as can be seen in her extraordinary naïve painting) once knelt to pick up a fallen napkin and was rewarded with a tap on the shoulder from a knifeblade and the unexpected words "Arise, Sir 'X'." In style, her work is not so far removed from that of Gertrude Halsband, except that the paint is a little looser; even Harrods is a long way from Somerset.

THE MERRY FOLKS CONCERT PARTY by April Kerr

Martin LEMAN

Martin Leman was born in London in 1934, the son of a Covent Garden fruit merchant. Following two years in the army, he trained and worked as a typographer. Until 1969, his main interest was chess, but then he started painting and this has occupied an increasing amount of his time, much of which is taken up by portrait commissions and requests to paint people's cats.

Besides his exhibitions at the Portal Gallery in London, his pictures have been shown in at least five other countries.

Nearly alone amongst British naïves he can claim to have harnessed a significant proportion of his work to the naughtiness of sex. His cats, flowers and ladies are all imbued with the same centrally-heated lush presentation.

His paint is smooth and he works carefully. The colour contrast is one of day-glo against velvety dark backgrounds.

He puts across the sex invitation in simple language. All his imagery is direct and compromising. The humour is keyhole humour, the invasion of the privacy of the boudoir.

SISTERS by Martin Leman

James LLOYD

James Lloyd was born in Alsager, Cheshire in 1905. He died in a small village near York in 1974. The passing of Lloyd was like the closing of a chapter. No Alfred Wallis. No Lloyd. (And now no Lowry.) A Götterdämmerung.

Lloyd, most of whose existence had been hard, taking on all kinds of jobs to keep a wife and family which at once stage included nine children, had for the last twenty years of his life watched his slow progress along the path to public esteem.

Coming from farming stock, Lloyd was fascinated with, and absorbed in painting, life on the land. It was from such pictures that, in the main, his reputation gradually grew. But it would be a cardinal error to dismiss him as an artist only concerned with the countryside and its creatures. There were many other sides to him, not all of them at first evident, and certainly not from a single encounter. His rich sense of humour, for instance, only crops up occasionally in his pictures and even then is not easy to define. It certainly has nothing to do with his keen (and weird) interest in notabilities—the Beatles, Lulu, Jean Shrimpton—of all of whom he made pictures. Nor could anyone guess what form a Lloyd painting might take. When he painted a picture of the well-known jockey Eddie Larkin, he showed him out fishing.

Then there was the Lloyd painting members of his family, or doing a triple-portrait of a French girl he had come to know well through a friend (a devastating performance in psychological understanding), or even the Lloyd producing his own version of St. George and the Dragon (and the maiden of course). Yet none of these Lloyds hint at yet another side to this complex artist. Behind the countryman, the drinker and gambler, the father of a big family, lay another almost secret Lloyd, barely perceptible.

James Lloyd, in his own private way, was a lyrical mysticist. If there was no yardstick by which to measure this personal vein of phantasy, there were always the paintings, the ones he made to illustrate glimpses

SELF-PORTRAIT AS ROUSSEAU by James Lloyd, 1967

THE THREE SHEEP by James Lloyd

into his other world. These words are written to try and say something about who Lloyd was. What follows concerns his work and the unique way in which he carried it out.

As an artist, he was a giant in many ways. The strain of his painstaking work method, and the huge output of pictures (perhaps two a month) especially from the late 1950s until the year of his death was both amazing and prodigious.

In effect, he had always wanted to make pictures. (He won a second prize in art when he was at school.) At seventeen he managed to sell one of his early black and white studies to a local policeman on condition that he made another one to match it. The combined price for both was one pound.

Trying to paint in the evenings after a long day out at work, he looked about him for some way in which he could emulate the great artists of the past. Constable and Turner he particularly admired, especially the former whose wonderful paintings of water he could only marvel at, never imitate.

Then, with a strange individual shrewdness, he "worked out" how to paint so that the colours of his pictures would have a genuine artistic flavour. Looking intensely at reproductions in books from the library, he realised that these (all in letterpress in those days, with offset litho yet to come) were printed from a series of "screens", one for each colour. A magnifying glass would show that all these illustrations of paintings were made up from hundreds of thousands of little coloured dots. It was the same with pictures in newspapers.

With patience, he could try for the same result.

"Dotty Lloyd" Ken Russell called him when he made the *Monitor* series television film about Lloyd and his work. (In fact this production turned out to be so successful that Russell made another television film, about the great Douanier Rousseau this time, and cast Lloyd who had never acted in his life in the starring rôle.) Television exposure, as has so

often since been the case, brought Lloyd and his curious pictures before a much wider public.

But it needs to be emphasised that the prime mover in starting his career as an artist was his wife Nancy. It was she who, after trying various ways to sell his pictures or have them shown in public, wrote to the art critic Sir Herbert Read who, with his colleague John Berger, went to see him and bought an armful of his pictures for £100, and Lloyd was so taken aback that he could not remember what pictures they took, or how many.

This visit led to his paintings being exhibited at the Arthur Jeffress Gallery in London and, later when Jeffress died, to his being taken up by the Portal Gallery.

It is true that he won prizes. His pictures were exhibited abroad. The Tate acquired his painting *Cat and Mouse* and, headed by the Duke of Bedford, a long line of collectors of Lloyd paintings came into being.

But somehow world recognition of his independent and eccentric talent matured too slowly. People, thousands of them, were overwhelmed by the velvety confluence of his myriads of coloured dots and how they gave a special quality to everything in the pictures—animals, vegetation, stonework, portraits, naked witches, pop stars—but the staid and important art establishment was not so fast to react. Only a year and a half before he died one of Lloyd's self-portraits was up for selection for an international portrait exhibition at Wildenstein Gallery (London). When the jury (all of them practising artists) were making their choice, one of its members, a noted academic painter, tried to have the Lloyd picture rejected on grounds that it was a printed reproduction and not a painting at all. Other jurors, with eventual success, set about disabusing him although a magnifying glass had to be produced to convince him finally.

Lloyd the painter, as can be seen, could have difficulties persuading professional artists about the autheticity of his vision and the unique way

in which he transferred it to painting.

There was fresh evidence of just how alert his keen and unsophisticated eyes could be during one of his day-trips to London. To stop him spending all his free time in pubs, Eric Lister got him to agree to see a film featuring his television favourites Morecombe and Wise.

During the first half of the programme, Lloyd was roisterous, admitting that he had not been to the cinema for twenty years and had never seen a film in colour; but later, when his two heroes arrived on screen, he became "technical" and observed: "They look much bigger than on telly; you see all the spots on their faces".

Lloyd paintings are generally small in size (their dimensions were governed by the size of the top of the kitchen table upon which he worked). Nearly all of his pictures are in private collections and museums. To the very last he kept up his pressure and could be found seven days a week seated in his cramped living room concentrating over one of his intricate works, oblivious to the television going full blast and several of his children and pets swarming around him.

Of his generation, he was the most important naïve artist living and working in Britain.

CHAMPION JOCKEY EDDIE LARKIN FISHING IN THE RIVER DERWENT by James Lloyd, 1962

Laurence Stephen LOWRY

Lloyd and Lowry were the two great names of the 1960s and 1970s. They knew each other, and were good friends upon the few occasions when they met. Of the two, Lowry was by far the best known to the public, but there the comparison ends, for Lowry, as he made perfectly clear to those who could not appreciate the fact for themselves, was never a naïve in the sense that Lloyd could be said to be. In fact there are purists who will say that he was not a naïve of any sort. Just the same, his particular form of vision and the way it came across the world at large suggested that, for all his experience and art training, he had a purity in his painting that is frequently associated with compulsive art especially in its naïve character.

Also, considering the enormous influence that Lowry's paintings have had upon so many naïve artists, particularly in the North, it is plain that no assessment of naïve art in Britain can overlook him or his contribution.

L. S. Lowry was born in 1887. He died in Salford in 1976.

In contrast with so many others mentioned in this book, Lowry, it should be realised, spent nearly ten years studying at Manchester School of Art. He had always wanted to be a painter and, at the beginning of his art career, he strove vigorously to become an academic artist. It was not really until the time when he left Manchester to take up residence in Salford (1909) that signs of the real and independent Lowry style began to appear in his work, and these were to take on recognisable and idiosyncratic form from 1915 onwards. A discerning few saw that a most intriguing artist had emerged, but the art world did not take stock of Lowry until his successful exhibition at the Alex Reid and Lefevre Gallery in London 25 years later.

From that year onward Lowry's reputation burgeoned and he rapidly became a desired and accepted painter by an increasing clientèle.

Not unreasonably Lowry, who happily had not had to face up to economic hardship in the intervening years, still felt that everything had happened a little too late. In fact, by the 1960s he was already complaining that having worked hard at painting all his life he was rapidly becoming

PLAYGROUND by L. S. Lowry, 1945

too tired to do much more (a confession he made to Sheldon Williams in a television interview at the Tate during his Arts Council retrospective exhibition in 1966).

But long before 1966 he had proved that he was an artist capable of painting many different kinds of subject even if all his pictures now bore the indelible stamp of his exceptional style.

There are his familiar begrimed *portraits* of the industrial North thronged with workers on their way to the shopfloor, returning home or spending what free time they are lucky to have at the markets, at the fair or attending public celebrations like the Coronation or VE Day. There is his warmhearted satire of beggars, freaks and "personalities" (like the bearded lady who sat opposite him in the train). And for Lowry so many of whose pictures are densely populated, there were also the empty Welsh landscapes and vistas of industrial cities outside Manchester (especially Huddersfield) presenting an urban face with factories but without artisans.

Apart from the more obvious and now famous hallmark of his style, what else could be said to distinguish this modern artist from his contemporaries?

Perhaps the most outstanding contribution he has made to the skills of painting has been his remarkable control and understanding of white pigment. Although itself the antithesis of a dirty industrialised society so often the subject of his work, he has been able to win from this non-colour a seemingly limitless range of effect and character. He once even made the experiment of covering a canvas with layer upon layer of white paint, leaving it for six years and then making the clinical comparison between it and another canvas also painted white which he left only for one day to dry. White (as Malevich discovered when he made his famous experimental painting *White on White*) has an incredible number of variations depending on age and state.

So what sort of an artist was Lowry, lover of the pre-Raphaelites (many of whose paintings and drawings he bought in sales for high prices), capable of a near total naïvety when he painted his few actual portraits for which the model sat, able to be bold or subtle, backed by nearly ten years of art training? One can only repeat that this lonely rebel has no equal, only imitators. A fine artist in his own exclusive right, he cannot be given a label, only a signature.

Toby LYON

Toby Lyon was born in 1926. For a while she attended art school at St. Ives, but that is a time she prefers to forget. Ever since she began to take painting seriously, her pictures have been purely intuitive. With a kind of inherent expertise she makes the grey atmosphere of Britain, especially along the seafront, like a quiet reminder of the eccentricities of the British sky. "Figures", as she describes them, occupy deck-chairs and gaze out to sea. The water may be calm or blustery. The openwork of the sky's clouds mimics the greys and near-blues of the sea beneath.

Toby Lyon does not allow the fat humour of Beryl Cook's paintings to enter her work. Her comedy is more throwaway, as for example the practical joke the wind plays when it blows the deck-chair inside out. Except for the chair's canvas stripes there are no bright colours. This is the world of Eastbourne and Bexhill painted with expert smooth assurance and with absolute feeling for situation comedy in sophisticated low-key.

FIGURES IN DECK CHAIRS by Toby Lyon

Jerzy MAREK

Jerzy Marek was born in Poland in 1925. He came to England in 1948 and now lives in Preston. He started painting in 1969 as a deliberately chosen contrast to exhausting office work. He has taken part in many local exhibitions and has shown his pictures in London and abroad.

Marek's work has now settled down into the neat and solidly painted style of naïvety so admired by the French. At one time people used to often feature in his pictures but, as in the case of those by Madge Gill, their faces were too often like simplistic self-portraits. Today he is more interested in painting birds and animals or inventing interiors of Victorian character. His work has strong ubiquitous appeal and is bought by a wide variety of people, by no means all of them classifiable as collectors.

SAM by Jerzy Marek, 1976

Moshe **MAURER**

Moshe Maurer was born in Brody, Russia in 1891. He grew up in a Jewish Hassidic society, the direct opposite of Liberal Jews. His principle interests were in music and writing humorous Yiddish verse. In 1914 he went to Holland and later to Belgium where he stayed until his escape to England in 1940. Ten years later he started to paint.

Exhibitions of his work have been held in London, Europe and the United States. In his paintings the Hassidic men wear their hair long in the traditional style together with curly sideburns and bushy beards. They usually wear widebrimmed black hats and silken overcoats; integration with the goyim is more for business than social reasons.

To the public he was a painter, working in dry colours with loose brush-strokes that made his pictures recognisably naïve although with a primitive accent.

But there was another Maurer, the paint manufacturer living in a repectable home in Finchley. This was the private person who, quite apart place in the art world, also painted on anything that took his fancy (generally upon things about the house). When Eric Lister went to see him one summer several years ago, Maurer poured him tea out of a painted teapot into a painted teacup on a painted teatable set before a roaring fire—painted of course by Moshe Maurer in the fireplace.

Hassidic Man by Moshe Maurer

Bill MAYNARD

Bill Maynard died prematurely in the early 1970s. He had not yet reached the age of forty. An intellectual, gifted with exceptional perception, he attended university but quit when he found the prevailing academic atmosphere unpalatable. For several years he occupied himself as a nomadic gardener during which time he carefully built up a fully classified and cherished collection of beetles.

He saw picture making as a communication system which could put into visual form thoughts, theories and eccentric ideas, all of them the product of his nonconformist mind. His was a kind of naïve intellectualism. Pre-dating the Pop Art boom, in many ways his paintings were exactly what Pop artists later tried to say.

It can be seen that even within the confines of his recognisable style he was a master of varieties (in both subject and composition). Sometimes his pictures with their clear lines and bright tints created a transformation of the contemporary world with accepted twentieth-century inventions turned into the monsters he believed they really were, or other pictures would show unbelievable maps and charts (sometimes close in appearance to a child's board of snakes and ladders).

Many of his works operate simultaneously upon different levels, but basically they are philosophical statements in which he calls for a complete overhaul of subjects like advertising, ecology, and sociology. Yet again, Maynard was also quite capable of painting voluptuous ladies looking as if they had just entered a religious life but could prove the validity of split personality by illustrating scenes from the Bible. Even amongst such a heterogeneous group as the artists of this book, he stands out for his offbeat talent and his intellectual performance, and because he was an original.

FAIRGROUND by Bill Maynard

Anthony MILLER

Anthony Miller was born in Stockport in 1914, and, having only one eye, has been confined to hospital since he was 6 years old. Unable to read or write, he communicates most impressively entirely in visuals. All his pictures, generally drawn on hardboard or shoe-boxes, have a tendency to rely on TV, what he sees around him, and the few glimpses he has of the world outside. Direct reality is limited by the fact that he rarely uses his working eye to record anything above ground or television-screen level.

Going to the Lights is a dazzling vision of the wonderful world outside hospital. Illiterate he may be, but to convey the artificial glitter of the Northern urban scene lit up with nothing more than a pencil and paper is no mean achievement.

Miller may have no better materials than so many Russian peasant naïves but he can turn them to far more magical effect. Do the words he tries to write on the shopfronts and the hoardings matter anyway? And the traffic . . .! The huge buses, juggernaut lorries, and so many cars of all sizes . . .! They could be illustrations for Patrick Hamilton's novel *Mr Stimpson and Mr Gorse* in which the author suggested that the whole world was in danger of turning into relentless lines of shiny black beetles.

GOING TO THE LIGHTS by Anthony Miller

Lewes MITCHELL

Lewes Mitchell, who was born in Penzance in 1932, believes he remembers his father working as a carriage cleaner at the terminus of the Great Western Railway. Lewes left school at the age of 15, having learnt to read and write, and went to work on a farm near St Ives for the next three years. He started painting in the late 1960s and of his work he says: "We were bloody poor, mother and sister and I. My pictures are what I am and to a lesser extent what my friends are, and even the street in Penzance I grew up in".

Today Lewes works in the earth moving business, and for the last ten years he has spent the evenings painting his pictures.

Mitchell's interests are ships, Mount's Bay, airplane patterns in the sky, and the patchwork of West Country fields with their wild flowers.

David Cross who shows his work at the Fine Art Gallery in Bristol first met the artist six years ago, a year after Nigel Gosling had arranged for some of Lewes Mitchell's paintings to be shown at the Grosvenor Gallery in London. Nearer home, this Bristol artist had not the same kind of success. The Newlyn Penzance Gallery turned him down because ". . . you are too bright for us Mr Mitchell".

He certainly is colourful. His simple direct imagery, often bordering on the decorative, has not much time for half-tones. The sea is blue unless the weather is bad, and then it becomes a vibrant murky hue. The rays from the lighthouse are white light. The sails of the two-master are Breton red with a sunflower design on one of them in brilliant yellow.

WRECK OF THE HILDA BROWN by Lewes Mitchell

Andrew MURRAY

Andrew Murray, grandson of Sir James Murray who edited the *Oxford English Dictionary*, was born in Tientsin, China in 1917. He did not start painting until he was thirty-nine. At that time he was working as a religious journalist in Cape Town. He had seven one-man shows of his work before his first exhibition in London at the Portal Gallery.

Murray became an artist almost by chance when a friend left him a box of oil paints, brushes and some canvasses. For a long while he did nothing with them. Then one day he started painting and taught himself what to do with his unusual inheritance.

As the son of two missionaries and gifted with a sense of humour he was able to see the comic element in many biblical stories. These were for some time the main stock from which he drew his inspirations, but in the intervening years he has become steadily more absorbed with the principle of *reconciliation*. For him, the lion should lie down with the lamb and in a kind of extension of the Franciscan theatre he has painted several portraits of himself in the rôle of the saint who sought to come to terms with the birds and the animals. He believes in reconcilation.

But now he has settled in Britain and has become even more concerned to make his guiding visual intention go to work in the urban jungle of London, a city he paints as if it had never suffered from smokeladen atmosphere or housed any criminals. Murray's London is clean, physically and morally. As far as he is concerned, reconciliation there has already taken place.

His style is straight naïve. Colours are bright even if the paint can sometimes be stodgy. Only his quirky humour (as in *First Communion and the Fierce Bull*) interferes with his otherwise serene vision.

ADAM NAMING THE ANIMALS by Andrew Murray, 1973

Halima NALEÇZ

Halima Naleçz was born in Wilno, Poland in 1917. She studied art at University with Stefan Batony, Professors Roube, Szyszko-Bogusz and Zahorska before becoming a student of H. J. Colson in Paris. This art training is emphasised because it makes all the more remarkable the development which her painting reached ten years ago. Since 1967 she has put aside all her previous art experience so that she can concentrate on what she describes as her "rediscovery of nature".

Something of her single-track ambition to paint a new version of nature can be seen in her 1969 *Summer Prelude* which formed part of her exhibition of The Four Seasons. Flowers are there in profusion. The whole canvas is full of them, except for the primitive bird flapping away in the top right hand corner.

Her solid paint has an almost cakelike consistency, but the colours are both delicate and rich in dramatic contrasts. Hers is a talent that has undergone total surgery, but the outcome of the operation is an innocence of vision that might never have known what the rest of the art world is doing. When not at her easel, her time is taken up running the Drian Art Galleries in London.

SUMMER PRELUDE by Halima Naleçz, 1969

Patricia NEVILLE

Patricia Neville was born in Colombo, Ceylon and is now in her late forties. Attending to her eight children has not deflected her from strenuous research into the lives of the British eccentrics. Since reading Edith Sitwell's book on the subject, knowing that she herself was no natural writer, she decided to turn her knowledge into painting. So from 1970 she set about teaching herself to paint. The result has proved positive.

Her pictures are certainly not perfunctory illustrations of a serious and wide-ranging investigation. Each painting tells a vivid and often grotesque story. Her style is one of cool naïve realism. Colours are subdued, almost as if they were as old as the people and scenes they portray. She has a natural flare for good composition which helps point up the eccentric behaviour and appearance of her motley cast of characters.

Currently living with her husband in Russia, she is busy preparing yet another exhibition of paintings of her British eccentrics.

She has already painted the mad Squire Mytton astride a bull ready for the Mytton hunt, with the bull in bit and bridle, swine-herd in attendance with the pigs who will serve as hounds. But there are so many more. How about Joey Grimaldi, the famous clown, chasing butterflies in gaudy costume while respectable lepidopterists watch with incredulity from the background?

Patricia Neville is an accomplished self-taught artist. She can make pictures of whatever her whim demands. It is the public's good fortune that she picked on such an extraordinary bunch of individualists to serve as models for her works.

SQUIRE MYTTON by Patricia Neville

Mary NEWCOMBE

Mary Newcombe was born in Harrow in 1922. She took a B.Sc. in natural sciences at Reading in 1943, and later taught mathematics and science in Somerset (until 1950). Although she never received any formal art training, she learned to draw and take visual stock of what took her fancy as potential subjects for paintings.

When she later moved with her husband to a small farm in Norfolk, the reaction to this change in lifestyle made itself evident in painting.

Besides exhibiting in London at the Leicester Galleries, the Beaux-Arts Gallery and Wildenstein Gallery, as well as having three one-man shows at the Crane Kalman Gallery, her pictures have been seen in France, Italy, Sweden and Holland.

The outstanding quality of her work lies in the way in which she is able to introduce into the most ordinary subject a surprise element, while simultaneously supressing anything that might suggest easy shock tactics. What goes for the subjects is also true of the colours. The paint may be laid on sparingly, almost casually, yet the impact is like that of a decisive hand in a silken glove.

THE TRIP BOAT by Mary Newcombe

Tom NEWMAN

During the second world war Tom Newman became a captain in the Grenadier Guards and, after serving in North Africa, took part in the Salerno landing in Italy. It was after the war that he took up painting and was able to show his pictures in three London galleries besides having works accepted, five years running, for the Paris Salon. He is a member of the Artistes Français de Paris, and lives in South Devon.

Newman's paintings have the look of eccentric timelessness about them. The simplicity and the purity of his imagery could almost be a legacy from ancient Egypt, and it is because of this archaic streak in his nature that he can rightly be classed as a primitive with his rough handling of paint and his near-casual delineation of detail. Colours tend to be pale, but the pigment is coarse. The images in his pictures are not difficult to recognise but they are all possessed of this dateless appearance. His is a brand of primitive phantasy from outside time.

ALICE IN CATLAND by Tom Newman

Barry O'CONNOR

Barry O'Connor was born in Nottingham in 1907. His father died when he was two years old. O'Connor, professional junk dealer, part-time poet and spiritualist, was forced to shut down his business because of traffic diversion. His mother had recently died at the age of 91. A man living close to the subsistence level and always having been a jack of all trades, he decided to have a try at painting and perhaps turn some of his pictures into a little money.

His hard life is in no way reflected in his lyrical (sometimes phantasist) paintings, deftly made in a style that comes somewhere between the direct imagery of the great French artist André Bauchant and that of the naïve charmers of fashionable self-taught in Paris today. At present it is difficult to get O'Connor to paint more pictures because he thinks he cannot get enough money from them. His eccentricity and hard way of life are best summed up in a short quotation from the man:

". . . Mother eked out a living as drawer, scalloper and jennier (out-worker in lace). In good times could earn two sovereigns for a sixteen-hour a day week.

. . . Lived well then (today a sovereign makes £28).

. . . Moved to Radford when a boy. . . . In bad times used to collect cobbles fallen off coal carts or sticks from the woods at Wollaton. Later hauled lace backwards and forwards from the Lace Market, left school at thirteen years, couldn't afford an apprenticeship with no wages, worked with bricklayers for 10/- weekly (wasn't allowed to pick up a trowel) and when sixteen years old found work as a Dyer's labourer (now called Dyer's Assistant); bad times in the early 30s earning £2 8s for a six hour day week. Used to collect a 1/- a week for Irish Sweep tickets to take to Dublin. Second time over paid in a winning ticket, Hyperion 1933, for the foreman who had a book from Ireland, worth £31,000. A fortnight later he gave me five shillings which I threw down in disgust and swore at him. Later threatened me if I ever took a course at College to better myself. . . . Sport, riding

horses, and in the show ring. Later smashed a leg badly—riding—was set wrong and second time in operating theatre surgeon said 'Have you any false teeth?' 'Yes'. 'If you've false teeth let's have 'em out then.' 'I can't take them out.' 'If you've false teeth, why can't you take 'em out?' 'Because I left 'em in the locker'. . . ."

These few words from O'Connor show the hapless man he has so persistently been. His pictures have been seen at Nottingham Playhouse and in the travelling exhibition of naïve artists which Christine McGegan arranged for the Arts Council in the West Midlands (1975–76).

THE LAST MAN ON EARTH by Barry O'Connor

Captain Michael O'NEIL

Michael O'Neil was born in Cork in 1888. Since becoming a widower in 1953 he has been living the life of a recluse in Formby (only seventeen minutes' walk from his ship's mooring in Liverpool), decorating the trees in his front garden with plastic oranges and lemons and—until he felt he had had enough—painting.

Painting enough pictures for Captain O'Neil meant filling a room with his pictures, three high on seven easels and covering all four walls except the corner where he stored coal. When the room was full, he stopped painting.

To give them extra depth, all his pictures were painted on double glass. The subjects were invariably ships, the sea and ports. The few who have been lucky enough to see his paintings agree that he displays great accuracy and has a remarkable talent. The problem has always been that O'Neil never wanted anyone to see his work, buy his pictures, least of all exhibit them in an art gallery. His excuse throughout has been fear of looting. Stories that had percolated through to him about the behaviour of ill-disciplined schoolchildren convinced him that if too much was known about his pictures the house would be raided.

No more paintings.

Instead he turned to making models of ships—again attractively precise in detail. Logic and eccentricity rarely go hand in hand. Captain O'Neil put his gallant vessels on display in the front window. No one has yet attempted to break into his house.

Captain Michael O'Neil never allowed any of his pictures to be photographed.

Bryan PEARCE

Bryan Pearce was born in St. Ives in 1929. He did not begin painting and drawing until he was 24. From 1954 until 1957, he attended the St. Ives School of Painting as a student of Leonard Fuller, ROI, RCA. Since that time he has painted only in watercolour. He has held fourteen one-man exhibitions of his work in Britain and his pictures have also been shown in Monte Carlo, Spotorno (Italy), Toronto and Belfast. Four television programmes about him and his work have been transmitted.

It is almost certain that if Pearce had not been an invalid since birth, he would not have turned to painting, or at least not in the same way. The irony is inescapable: his misfortune has been our reward.

At the very start there was reasonable doubt about how his interest in making paintings would develop. The early pictures were uncertain, too close to the outcome of therapy to qualify as more than "happy accidents". Their make-up was random and haphazard. It was as if some tachiste spirit from the world outside Cornwall had invaded St. Ives. Nevertheless, in their stirring way, they were certainly interesting.

Then his style developed.

He started chronicling St. Ives with almost the same enthusiasm for detail as Utrillo had for Paris. Like Dixon, he sometimes painted views of the landscape from overhead. For him St. Ives was as much a carpet as a port. Like Vivin, he featured the bricks of the buildings in his paintings. His colours are the bright clay tints of the bricks, green where there is grass, and the bright blues of sky and sea. Sunshine predominates.

COALBOAT WITH PALE BLUE FUNNEL IN ST IVES HARBOUR by Bryan Pearce

Bryan Pearse

Henry PERRY

Henry Perry, who used to live in Surbiton, was born in 1902 and died c.1970. His paintings only date from the last twelve years of his life, finding the work hard because of his arthritis.

The quiet-natured Perry started by making his pictures on paper and cardboard, framing the results with strips of rough wood. He always believed firmly in the basic values of good straightforward raw materials and to the end he ground his own colours.

In his style of painting, he came closest to John Deakin. Both had chosen to paint people, although Perry liked to show them clad in Edwardian dress and favoured the soft tones of a wispy almost impressionist background rather than the dark settings or careful chequerboard against which Deakin liked to range his models. Where their pictures find their closest parallel is in the faces and poses of the portraits.

SMALL PORTRAIT by Henry Perry, 1965

PIC (Tearlach S. Higgins)

PIC was born of Scottish parents in Belgrano near Buenos Aires in 1893. By 1906, he was at Malvern College (which he hated) and then went on to London University to take an engineering degree. He fought in the first world war and was wounded at Gallipoli. Immediately after the war, he returned to South America.

PIC (he has long discarded the name Higgins) married the artist Kate Elizabeth Olver in 1930. When they went to live in Barra in the Outer Hebrides they were both painting. That was the same year as his first exhibition (Wertheim Galleries) since which time he has had a number of one-man shows (Wertheim 1932, Matthiesen 1939, the Modern Art Gallery 1944, 1945, 1946, seven exhibitions at Gimpel Fils, Centaur Gallery 1961, Reid Gallery 1963, Alwin Gallery 1968 and 1970). His pictures have also been seen in Paris and Rome. Besides his painting, PIC has also written, using the pseudonym Ian Dall, three books of verse, a travel book about Aran Island, and *Sun Before Seven*, an autobiography of his early life in South America.

As a painter, PIC is on the outer edge of the contemporary scene, unconnected with any style or movement. His pictures, generally small, propose a wonderland whose inhabitants rarely betray any resemblance to bird, fish or mammal. His phantasy colours tend to be on the sombre side but with the luminosity of stained glass. The paintings themselves are not difficult to interpret. They may have the occasional splurge of colour (reminiscent of certain pictures by Max Ernst), but however bizarre the imagery, they are extremely easy on the eye.

DREAM OF A BIRDWATCHER by PIC, 1961

Alan PINDER

Alan Pinder was born in 1917 and died in the Dordogne in 1976. After a short and unrewarding time at the Central School of Arts and Crafts, London, he showed his work at a number of London galleries (Wertheim, Ward, Leger, Redfern, Modern Art, and the Artists' Patrons). His pictures were also seen in France at the Galerie Zak, the Galerie Antoinette and with the Surindépendants de France. Examples of his work are to be found in several international museums.

After much experimenting, he turned to his own interpretation of naïve vision during the early 1940s, and he remained true to this style of painting until his death. As the years rolled by some of the original crudity of his work was gradually ironed out. Like Lloyd, he favoured a fine-tipped brush, although he did not use it to fill up every area of the painting with tiny stippling. His favourite subjects—landscapes, beaches, seascapes and small town rural scenes—are sometimes invaded by figures from Greek and Roman mythology. His colours are gaudy, asserting that Eden was brightly decorated.

DIANA AND ACTAEON IN FOUR POSITIONS by Alan Pindar

George PINDER

George Pinder was born in Manchester in 1895. When he retired in 1962 he took up painting. He works on his pictures in the early morning and spends the rest of the day walking or in the garden. This *Candide* life suits him very well, although it is interesting to note that the landscape he prefers to paint has little of the quality of the pictures which include people. (People, he says, are not very easy to paint.)

The Ball is a fine crowded picture by George Pinder. Twenty-one couples and a few unattached figures looking for partners were the best possible raw material for one of his successful paintings. Bandstand, two massive archways, one square and one curved, and the art nouveau pretence of interior decoration add up to a delightful if absurd frivolity.

George Pinder paints carefully, everything is just so, although he has complete indifference to distance and perspective.

THE BALL by George Pinder

Joe SCARBOROUGH

Joe Scarborough was born in Pitsmoor, Sheffield in 1938. He was brought up in Fitzallen Street and this landscape of terraced houses was to dominate his future painting.

He made his first pictures when he was sixteen years old (copying illustrations of the Impressionists and the ship pictures by Montague Dawson from books in the public library). He worked in the pit at Thorpe Hesley Colliery for seven hours a day and maintained that the blinding light of day when he came back to the surface confirmed the truth of Impressionism. He also asserts that from early on he was deeply affected by the American artists John Sloan and George Luks.

When Scarborough started painting seriously he found he could hold exhibitions of his pictures in local clubs and pubs, but it was when he met his agent Cyril Caplan at his exhibition in the Crucible Theatre, Manchester (a sell-out in five hours) that his career really began. Today, he is a full-time painter and has built up a reputation for his work, especially in and around Sheffield.

Whatever he learnt from the Impressionist has been set aside. In feeling his pictures are much closer to the posters of Beggarstaff, except that they are far more complicated and the colours are like a memory of Turkish Delight (or even Harrogate Toffee). On another level, he could be said to be a bit brasher than the late Harold Gilman, but just as multi-hued. His thick paint is appreciated by a world escaping the revival of Aubrey Beardsley and art nouveau. There is a small element of caricature present. Shoes are too big. Young men do not sit astride motorcycles; they straddle them.

Scarborough points up the astonishing partnership of artist and pro-moter in the North. Of Cyril Caplan he says, "he has guided me into the professional world. Our relationship is more like that of patron and painter as in the Renaissance period".

THE TEMPERANCE BAR by Joe Scarborough

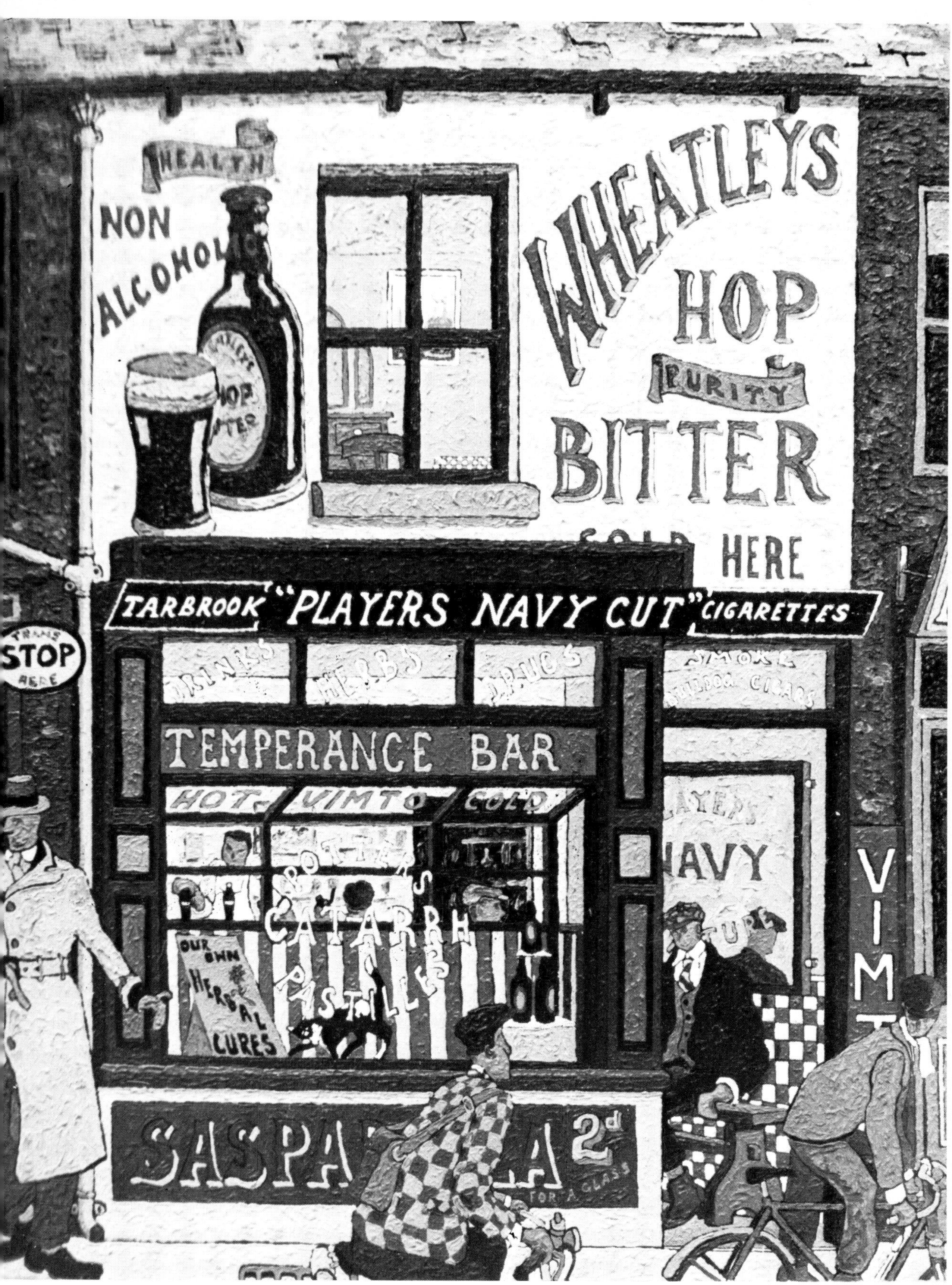
HEALTH
NON ALCOHOLIC
HOP BITTER
WHEATLEYS HOP
PURITY
BITTER
HERE
TARBROOK "PLAYERS NAVY CUT" CIGARETTES
STOP
DRINKS HERBS DRUGS
SMOKE
CIGARS
TEMPERANCE BAR
HOT VIMTO COLD
POTTERS
CATARRH PASTILLES
OUR OWN HERBAL CURES
PLAYERS NAVY
VIM
2d
FOR A GLASS

Alan SMITH

Alan Smith was born in Lemington, Northumberland in 1929. In 1952 he joined the West Riding Police Force and is now a detective officer.

He did not take a real interest in painting until he was forty years old, but between 1970 and 1975 he has taken part in fourteen exhibitions. His style is recognised for its hard precision. He likes his buildings to stand out in lonely eminence against a sky of cold authority in the Pennines at the close of the year. This is stern reality, beautifully composed. In his own words, "I see Winter as symbolic of our society today. . . . The low sun has a way of simplifying shapes in landscapes. I particularly enjoy the effect of light on texture such as stone walls and buildings . . .".

YORKSHIRE MOORS by Alan Smith

Don SMITH

Don Smith was born in Worksop in 1926. He took a clerical course during the five years he was with the RAF and then he took up several dull office jobs (from 1966 onwards, mostly in London). For eight years, especially the last three, he strove to master the art of painting with indifferent success.

In 1973 he saw—for the first time—the works of Raoul Dufy and, realising what the late Frenchman could achieve, especially in pictures related to sporting events, he decided to try and translate his own enthusiasm for sport into painting. His sporting pictures have been seen in seven exhibitions in the North and have appeared in three exhibitions in London.

He paints his subjects with a fine brush in what almost amounts to a dense stipple. The pictures are mainly of football and rugger matches, but he also does paintings of cricket, motor racing and events like the Oxford and Cambridge Boat Race.

Although it seems to him that such occasions are near to an excuse to concentrate upon the tangled masses of the thousands of supporters on the terraces and grandstands, paintings like *The First Division* still find room for the game itself and the same is true of *Lianag, Vernon's Cup-winner 1975* with the jockeys doubled over their mounts for the final spurt. (There is a note on the back of the racing picture, "The 'plane awaits winning jockey Yves St. Martin to return him to Paris".)

THE FIRST DIVISION by Don Smith

Sam SMITH

Sam Smith was born in 1908. Originally an architect, he retired early from what had been a comfortable career so that he could amuse himself, and others, with the quirky fabrications of his lively imagination.

For the Establishment, Smith was for a long time difficult to accept. His wit and irreverence were disturbing. His pictures and his adult toys did not seem serious enough for lazy stodgy minds and blasé eyes.

When he bought an abandoned golfcourse in Devon and went to live in the clubhouse, he effectively turned his back on the tedious squabble about his viability as an artist. There were enough discerning people (buyers and collectors of his work) unaffected by this aesthetic snobbery. He did not need plaudits from the others.

Smith was probably the first to recognise the savour of nostalgia; at least forty years before anyone else he began making a collection of seaside postcards, and more than twenty years ago he hit upon what was then a unique diversion, inventing his own comic strip cartoon free from rules and editing.

Many of Smith's toys were automatons or hand manipulative. They were often full of visual puns and other surprises. During the same period he made simple things as well, objects like the *mood-indicators*, two-sided wooden peg-style heads which could be twisted to show Grumpy on one face, Happy on the other.

Using a mixture of irony and slapstick, this artist debunks every accepted legend or platitude. Currently he is engaged upon two major projects: "classical weddings" (between centaurs and centauresses) commissioned by the Department of Education and Science to demonstrate to the public *how to be your own craftsman*, and the concept for the new shopping centre at Lewisham boasting a clock, complete with animated figures as its centrepiece.

By the mid-1970s, Sam Smith had acquired total public recognition for the fine and original artist he is, although he had already had several successful exhibitions in the United States before he was 'discovered' in Britain.

A MOOD-INDICATOR by Sam Smith

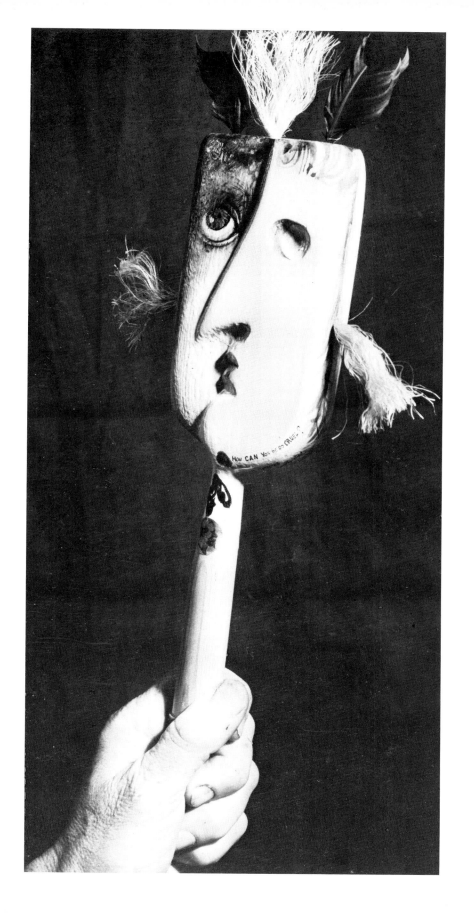

Henry STOCKLEY

Henry Stockley was born at the turn of the century. His father had been a sign-writer and two of his uncles had worked in stained glass. Perhaps these three in some way explain how Henry Stockley, the Green Line ex-busdriver became an artist.

It was the redoubtable Mrs Wertheim (who took chances with so many new artists, often successfully but by no means always) who discovered that, besides his work on the Green Line coaches and despite a wife who was firmly anti-art, he was also a busy and bustling painter, and it was she who organised an exhibition of his paintings at her London galleries in 1937.

Stockley painted with primitive enthusiasm in a simple naïve style which combined emotion and vision. His reception by the general public may not have been ecstatic, but it was sufficiently warm for Mrs Wertheim to include his works in several other exhibitions.

About his painting *Trafalgar Square*, *News Review* wrote 17 February 1938, "a pleasant work with grey-white blossoms and birds predominating, with a nondescript feeding two or three of the pigeons . . .".

CONEYS by Harold Stockley, 1933

Ben SUNLIGHT

Ben Sunlight was born in Brighton in 1935. He was awarded a diploma for Mural Painting by the Central School of Art and Design (London 1962). He lives in London and Whitstable. His work has been seen in four one-man exhibitions in London, and in 1972 he received the gold medal for art from the International Academy of Literature, Art and Science (Tommaso Campanella) of Rome.

This artist belongs to the tatterdemalian fringe of Britain's sophisticated naïves. Despite much technique and long background training, his independence of vision, particularly in the composition and simplicity of his nude studies, should not be overlooked. Sunlight makes patterns easily acceptable to the eye. He is never out to dazzle or bewilder. His tones, pale for figures, darker for backgrounds, have the same antique values as those of archaic terracottas and vases.

PERSUASION by Ben Sunlight

NAÏVE REALIST·

Douglas Edward TAYLOR

Douglas Edward Taylor, now in his late forties, was born in Battersea. Today he lives in a Gloucestershire village. This quiet serious man was originally apprenticed in the old craft of church carpenter. War and the disastrous fish emporium he started with the money from his postwar gratuity have long since returned him to his original trade, except that now he is a joiner instead of the traditional church carpenter. During the 1950s he started painting.

Douglas Edward Taylor paints slowly. Carried out with painstaking care, his pictures end up looking like personalised Victorian oleographs except that they have an eerie atmosphere of quality totally lacking in that kind of Victoriana. They also have a special naïvety not to be found in the work of any other painter of any other period. This is the appearance of their style—not their content, and certainly not their impact.

Douglas Edward is a remarkable artist in the true sense of the word. The snag about his works, if there is one, is that they are so exceptional. He is an artist for purists and all those who have real respect for independence of vision.

SITTING IN THE FRONT PARLOUR by Douglas Edward Taylor

Jack TAYLOR

Jack Taylor was born in London's East End in 1938. Taking all kinds of jobs, some of them amounting to casual labour, his existence (also interrupted by the time he deserted from military service) for a long period seemed to him pointless. The story goes that when he was in his twenties working as a road repairer outside the Redfern Gallery in Cork Street, Mayfair, one of his mates spurred him on to have a word with the gallery's director who was rearranging the street showcase. He claimed in no uncertain terms that he could paint better pictures than the ones on show. The director, who had no doubt heard this story from many other artists in the past, cynically replied "OK. If that's how you feel, please bring your paintings in". When Taylor eventually brought his pictures to the gallery, much to the director's surprise, the reaction was favourable. In fact the director was so impressed that he arranged an exhibition for Taylor and this turned out to be completely successful.

Despite this auspicious beginning, once Taylor had proven his point, he disappeared from the art scene for many years, and it was not until the mid-1960s that he reappeared. Since that time he has had two further exhibitions.

Taylor, when the enthusiasm grips him, can paint and sculpt thirty-six hours at a stretch. (Since his first Redfern exhibition, he has been firing clay he collects from bombsites). His near-illiteracy seems to have in no way diminished his ability and the range of his imagination. To see the artist talking to himself, look at *Stretched Painter* which although only twenty inches across, tells in phantasist terms how Taylor can feel himself trapped in his own canvas, prisoner of desires that prevent him from taking his ease in the comfortable world of realistic academic painting.

STRETCHED PAINTER by Jack Taylor

Romaine **TIMAEUS**

Romaine Timaeus was born in Westminster in 1926. For the past twelve years she has lived in Putney, during all of which time she has been painting. She is now a local Justice of the Peace.

Working slowly and with much deliberation, she has moved from straight and detailed naïve paintings on to a more sophisticated level where she plots complex compositions and is no longer afraid of sharper contrasts of colours. Many of her paintings have as their subject matter the suburban Thames-side environment where she lives and even her paintings of rural themes have a quality of urban bourgeois realism, reminiscent of the work of Louis Vivin. There is, for instance, a hint of suburbia in a painting like *Fishing Tackle, Cei Newydd*. Everything is neatly stacked. Ships' ropes are as taut as a cat's cradle. Only nature is allowed to get a little out of hand, but where else are leaves so beautifully arranged? As her exhibition at the Upper Street Gallery in Islington was to prove, her direct craftsmanship always brings her respect.

Mwnt Church Mwnt by Romaine Timaeus

William **TOWERS**

William Towers was born in Preston in 1935 and now lives in Leicester-shire. Over many years he has made himself adept at knitting and making rugs and patchwork quilts, but he only began making his quilted pictures in 1970. At first he relied on biblical subjects, but subsequently, like so many other naïve artists, he changed to working upon pictures of childhood memories. As with Elizabeth Allen, although sharing none of her exotic inspirations, his fabric collage is his working method and bears no relation to his quilts of the past, except in its skill.

GOODNIGHT, GOD BLESS by William Towers, 1975

Alfred WALLIS

Alfred Wallis (1855–1942) was born at North Corner, Devonport. His father was a master paver and his mother came from the Scilly Isles. Wallis himself was believed, though this is not corroborated, to have worked with the St. Ives fishing fleet which often made the trip to the North Sea, and there is even the story that he once crossed the Atlantic to Newfoundland and suffered shipwreck. Living first in Penzance and then moving to St. Ives, he did not start painting until 1922, three years after the death of his wife. (She had been twenty years his senior.)

Although Ben Nicholson and Christopher Wood (who admitted to being strongly influenced by Wallis's pictures) discovered him in the late 1920s, it was not until 1962—twenty years after his death—that he had his first one-man show in London (Piccadilly Gallery, July 1962) and although today he has won his spurs as a world master of primitive painting with his pictures in international museums including the Tate Gallery and New York's Museum of Modern Art, such recognition is very belated for the ex-fisherman turned artist and religious maniac.

H. S. Ede wrote of him, "Alfred Wallis is *the* Primitive painter of the twentieth century and I know of no other so essentially Primitive in the sense of the great Cave painters". This artist covered his pictures with black cloth on Sundays because he felt his beautiful paintings of ships and coastline interfered with the Sabbath, believing them to be Graven Images, which his favourite book the Bible preached against. He said of them "the most you get is what used to be, all I do is out of my memory, I do not go out anywhere to draw. It is what I have seen before. I paint things what used to be, and there is only one or two what has them, and I does no harm to anyone". It can be seen from these remarks that he loved the old Cornwall he felt and saw being destroyed before his eyes. Artist or no, he wanted to make pictures "out of my memory" before it was too late.

Wallis, like Dixon and Pearce, often painted as if viewing everything from overhead, but in his way his eccentric perspective was even more

at odds with the camera's eye than theirs. And like Dixon, he used any materials that came to hand, the old brushes for painting boats, discarded paint at the bottom of cans, the tops and bottoms of cardboard boxes, sometimes cut by him into irregular shapes to suit the subject he intended to paint on them.

Ben Nicholson and Christopher Wood got on well with him, but normally he kept the list of his friends down to a minimum. After his wife's death, he felt pictures and the Bible were enough for him ("I am a Bible-keeper it is Red three hundred and sixty times a year by me and that is everyones Duty").

The colours in Alfred Wallis paintings are "plain" like their subjects, but colour and picture itself are all imbued with a fierce beauty. There is no decoration; every simple image appears ungarnished and vital in its own right. His paintings are truly the product of primitive emotion.

SAILING BOATS by Alfred Wallis

Chris WARE

Chris Ware was born in 1904 in Aldershot, Hampshire. He was educated at the Silesian College in South Farnborough. During the second world war he worked as a photographer aboard destroyers in the Royal Navy. All his paintings relate to France of which he has fond memories from childhood, especially Brittany and Normandy which he and his wife visited as soon as the war was over.

Although he has only been painting for the past six or seven years, as if to make up for lost time, he works like one possessed. Some of the canvases are on the large side, some of them small, but all of them capture the Celtic world beyond the sea, or the backstreets of Paris, or even village life on the Côte d'Azur. The paint is lively and vivid, with plenty of energy and action. Horses move, people move, even the buildings seem to move. In another place and at another time he could have been a sort of Soutine with a naïve accent. Definitely in love with France, he has an unexpected authentic feeling for that foreign country.

His pictures were shown at Gallery 359, Nottingham and as part of the Last Man on Earth Arts Council exhibition of naïve art organised by Christine McGegan, a large collection which toured the cities of the West Midlands.

St Ann La Palud (detail) by Chris Ware

John WATNEY

Having reached comfortable middle age, John Watney finds time to work as an executive for charities. He has also been responsible for some well-made naïve paintings.

Watney has done an important job of work on behalf of autistic children, he is well versed in the complications of exotic art, and he also has the right kind of natural gift to paint a picture like *My Mother in her Talbot-Darracq*. If the picture of Mother sounds almost like an invasion of Neil Davenport country, it should be pointed out that John Watney's painting is carried out in a series of sepia tints so that it has more the appearance of a faded photograph than a picture in oils.

He paints exactly what he wants to convey. His pictures are clear in his mind and he wants them to appear just as clearly in paint. Like Davenport, he enjoys painting pictures of a luxury world that has vanished into the past.

MY MOTHER IN HER TALBOT-DARRACQ by John Watney

Ted WILLCOX

Ted Willcox was born in Brentford in 1909. He spent much of his life in Turnham Green, Middlesex. His main employment has been as a night-watchman. He is a quiet man, too easily lost in the crowd. His social life centres round the local pub.

He became a naïve artist by accident. After he was injured during service with the RAF in wartime, and following a spell in hospital, he went to a convalescent home where he and his colleagues were encouraged to take up a manual therapy. A number of them, including Willcox, chose embroidery and appliqué.

At the start, Willcox followed the general trend which was to work on embroidering coats of arms and RAF insignia, but his inborn impulse persuaded him to try more interesting subjects like *Anne Hathaway's Cottage*.

In 1944, he took a more decisive step and reproduced his own pin-up *Marlene Dietrich* from a photograph. Thereafter he concentrated upon pin-ups, although he also made an embroidery of Lee Harvey Oswald being shot by Jack Ruby and it was this "picture" which Vincent Smith, at work upon decorating a room for Peter Blake, showed the famous pop artist who immediately wanted to see more. Vincent Smith lived in the same block of flats as Willcox, so a meeting was easily arranged. What Blake saw was a room draped with pin-ups as dated as the Varga girls out of old copies of *Esquire* taking their place alongside the "portraits" of familiar figures like Betty Grable, Alice Faye and Rita Hayworth. All of them were carefully stitched in garish Willcox colours upon linen tea towels.

Blake told the Portal Gallery. An exhibition called the Private Pin-Ups of Ted Willcox was arranged. If this had taken place in the 1970s its effect might have been very different. A number of critics were impressed (Robert Melville bought one); those who came to the gallery liked them but, in most instances, there the matter rested. There was not the expected burst of public enthusiasm.

Among the few who did realise the unique value and beauty of Ted Willcox's embroideries, the American humorist S. J. Perelman stands out. He was so fascinated with them that he wrote a short story for the *New Yorker* about a tea-towel artist.

PIN-UP silk embroidery by Ted Willcox

Florence **WILLIAMS**

Florence Williams was born in Everton, Liverpool in 1893. When she was twelve years old she worked in a Lancashire cotton mill where she trained as a weaver and was later able to use her acquired skill at Harris's Mill, Cockermouth, Cumberland. But when it looked as if she might be laid off, she left to take up work as a cook general in domestic service. There were good openings for this kind of employment in Australia and she spent some time on that side of the world before returning once again to Britain work as temporary cook at a number of different houses.

Three years before the second world war she bought a cottage and it was here that she started her rug-making. Her little home needed floor coverings, but of her first rugs she says "I don't like to remember them; they were dreadful".

From the cottage, she was able to take up the job of village post-mistress and it was during this period that she was mugged and consequently has, since that time, been very nervous of any publicity. But it was also during her post office employment that she encountered the designer Nancy Peel who asked her if she knew anyone who made rugs. The meeting with Nancy Peel was really the beginning of her career as a naïve artist. From then on her reputation grew. Using offcuts of Otterburn tweed as her raw materials she was able to create an almost Impressionist brilliance in her woven pictures, so different from the patch-work short-cut methods or the gros-point nature of the output of so many other rug-makers.

The weaving of her naïve picture rugs give life purpose, she declares. How she goes about her work is uncomplicated and forthright, but if she is not quite certain about details of any of the subjects in her pictures, she goes to the local library and checks up on the facts.

RAM RUG by Florence Williams

SCOTTIE WILSON

Scottie was born in Glasgow in 1890. He died in 1974. Not surprisingly, his origins are presumed to be Scottish although there is a rumour that the family originally were Jewish serfs in Poland who, when they gained their liberty, and not without conscious irony, took the name Freeman. It is the kind of story that fits in well with Scottie's character. He is one of the supreme originals in the history of modern British art.

He did not start making his extraordinary pictures until the mid-1930s when he was in Toronto (after numerous vicissitudes like buying himself out of the Army in Bloemfontein in 1911).

Scottie Wilson, the son of a taxidermist's assistant, turned out to be the modern master of the stuffed fish and the bird caught in frozen attitude—all in a world free of perspective whose only human intervention appeared in masks and headpieces that seemed to owe their inspiration to Maori tattooing but were actually culled from his knowledge of the North American Indians. Scottie's works were so amazing in their phantasy that he was chosen to be represented in Jean Dubuffet's "Collection" in *L'Art Brut*.

His pictures fall into two categories; the earliest and those that most people consider the best were drawn in indian ink and tinted with cool-tone watercolours, but later he frequently used thick opaque gouache colours on dark paper. Either way, the imagery drawn from his select number of subjects did not waver—fish, swans, exotic plant life, masks and magical faces, sometimes butterflies, and nearly always dense linear decorations of every form as fine and carefully worked out as the grain from the cross-cut of some ancient tree. Scottie Wilson could be said to have built a new world somewhere between sweet dreams and nightmare, except that no other person could ever imagine their sleep being disturbed in quite that way.

Scottie's personality matched his individuality of artistic style. When he could afford it, he lived on whiskey, kippers and Woodbines and, if temporarily he was better off, he would have cloth caps and boots made

up for him in Savile Row.

In times when Savile Row was out of the question, he pared down his activities to a far more prosaic level. People who came to see Goering's Mercedes-Benz in Oxford Street found an exhibition of Scottie's pictures going on in an empty shop next door. At a seaside resort he even hired a tent to be put up on the promenade. The pictures hung inside the tent. Outside stood a notice "Famous Artist—Scottie Wilson—Exhibition—Admission 3d". He made himself into a sideshow for trippers.

As a pure and unique phantasist artist, he had only one off-colour interlude during his art career, when he designed a china set for Royal Doulton. All the subject matter was pure Scottie, but somehow the vital element of his originality seemed unable to enter what was essentially a commercial project.

VILLAGE BIRDS AND FISH by Scottie Wilson

MISS WONDERLEE by Martin Leman

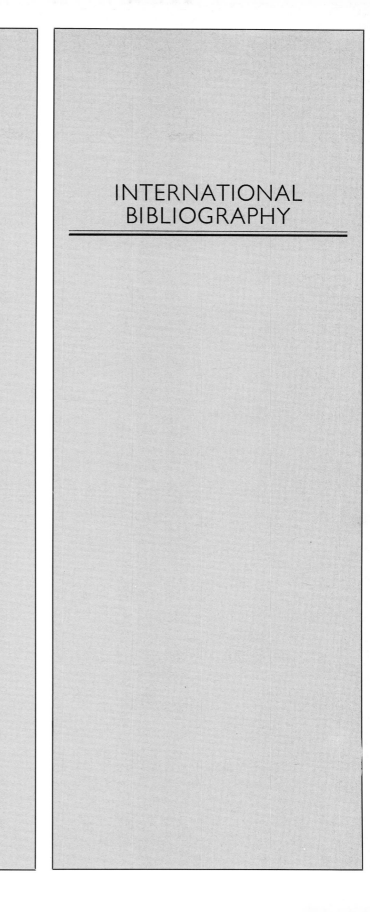

INTERNATIONAL
BIBLIOGRAPHY

Books

Adam, L., *Primitive Art*, 3rd ed., Harmondsworth 1954

Art populaire: travaux artistiques et scientifiques du Ier Cong. int. des arts populaires (Prague 1928), 2 vols, Paris 1931

Artieri, Giovanni, *L'opera completa di Rousseau il doganieri*, Milan 1969

Bašičević, Dimitrije, *Ivan Generalić*, Zagreb 1962

Bašičević, M., ed., *Les primitifs yougoslaves*, Dubrovnik 1956

Basler, Adolphe, *Henri Rousseau, sa vie, son oeuvre*, Paris 1927

Beier, Ulli and Bihalji-Merin, Lise, *Henri Rousseau: Leben und Werk*, Dresden 1971

Bigiaretti, Libero, *Orneore Metelli*, Invrea 1964

Bihalji-Merin, Oto, *Das naïve Bild der Welt*, Cologne 1959 (Eng. trans. N. Guterman *Modern Primitives: masters of naïve painting*, London, New York 1961)

—— *Ivan Generalić*, Baden-Baden 1960

—— *Modern Primitives: naïve painting from the late seventeenth century until the present day*, London 1971

—— *Primitive Artists of Yugoslavia*, New York 1964

—— *Yugoslavian Primitive Art*, Belgrade 1959

——, Lise and Oto, *Leben und Werk des Malers Henri Rousseau*, Dresden 1971

Bing-Bodmer, H., *Camille Bombois*, Paris 1951

Boas, Franz, *Primitive Art*, New York 1955

Bouret, J., *Henri Rousseau*, Neuchâtel 1961

Bradley, Helen, *And Miss Carter Came with Us*, London 1973

—— *And Miss Carter Wore Pink*, London 1971

Buccarelli, Palma, *Orneore Metelli*, Rome 1946

Cahill, Holger, Gauthier, Maximilian and others, *Masters of Popular Painting*, New York 1938

Cardinal, Roger, *Outsider Art*, London 1972

Carraher, Ronald G., *Artists in Spite of Art*, New York 1970

Certigny, Henry, *La vérité sur le douanier Rousseau*, Paris 1961

—— *La vérité sur le douanier Rousseau, Addenda numéro 2: Le conseil municipal de Paris et les artistes indépendants*, Lausanne, Paris 1971

—— *Le douanier Rousseau et Frumence Biche*, with a preface by Anatole Jakovsky, Lausanne, Paris 1973 (Eng. trans, Benita Eisler)

Chassé, Charles, *Dans les coulisses de la gloire: d'Ubu roi au douanier Rousseau*, Paris 1947

Cocchiara, G., *L'eterno selvaggio: presenza e influsso del mondo primitivo nella cultura moderna*, Milan 1961

Collis, Maurice, *The Discovery of L. S. Lowry*, London 1951

Courthion, Pierre, *Henri Rousseau*, Geneva 1944

—— *Orneore Metelli, le peintre cordonnier*, Geneva 1951

Dansk Kulturhistorisk Museumsforening, Copenhag *De naesten ukendte . . . skilderier fra 1800-årene*, 1971

D'Arbeloff, Natalie and Yates, J., *Creating in Colle* London 1967

Dasnoy, Albert, *Exégèse de la peinture naïve*, Brussels 19

Denvir, Bernard (and others), *Salon Mondial de la Peint Naïve*, Salon Levallois-Perret 1975

Deonna, Waldemar, *Du miracle grec au miracle chréti classiques et primitivistes dans l'art*, Basle 1945–48

—— *Primitivisme et classicisme: les deux faces de l'histoire l'art*, Paris 1946

Depouilly, Jacques, *Enfants et primitifs*, Neuchâtel 1964

Descargues, Pierre, *Le douanier Rousseau*, Geneva 1972

Dubuffet, Jean, *Asphyxiante culture*, Paris 1971

—— *Prospectus et tous écrits suivants, I and II*, Paris 196

Duca, Lo, *Henri Rousseau dit le douanier*, Paris 1951

Fourny, Max, *Le Chanson Traditionelle et les Na Musee d'Art Naïf de l'Ile de France*, 1976

Gamulin, G., *Les peintres naïfs: école de Hlebine*, Paris 19

Garçon, Maurice, *Le douanier Rousseau, accusé naif*, Pa 1953

Gauthier, Maximilian, *André Bauchant*, Paris 1943

—— *Henri Rousseau*, Paris 1949

Geist, H. F., *Carl Christian Thegan aus Oldesloe. I Laienmalerei, ein Grenzebiet der Kunst*, Flensburg 19

Goldwater, R. J., *Primitivism in Modern Painting*, N York, London 1938

Grey, Roch, *Henri Rousseau*, Paris 1943

Grochowiak, Thomas, *Werk und Werkstatt naiver Kur Städtische Kunsthalle*, Recklunghausen, 1971

Jakovsky, Anatole, Ces peintres de la semaine de s dimanches, introduction to *La peinture naïve: douanier Rousseau à nos jours*, Knokke-Zoute 1958

—— *Gaston Chaillac*, Paris 1952

—— *La peinture naïve*, Paris 1949

—— *Les peintres naïfs*, Paris 1956

—— *Louis Vivin: peintre de Paris*, Paris 1952

—— *Peintres naifs: lexique des peintres naïfs du mo entier*, Basle 1967; new ed, 1976

Janis, Sidney, *They Taught Themselves: American pri tive painters of the Twentieth Century*, New York 19

Jasmand, Bernhard, *Sonntagsmaler: das Bild des Einfälti Herzens*, Berlin 1956

Jones, Ruth, *The Path of the Son* (Bryan Pearce), Sherlc Gallery Publications, Sherlock near Tor Point, 197(

Keleman, Boris, *Naïve Art: paintings from Yugosla* (in press)

—— *Yugoslav Naïve Painting*, Zagreb 1969

Kolle, Helmud, *Henri Rousseau*, Leipzig 1922 (*Ju Kunst*, vol. 27)

Kühn, H. *Die Kunst der Primitiven*, Munich 1923

Larkin, David, ed., *Innocent Art*, London 1974

—— *Rousseau*, New York 1975

vy, Mervyn, *Drawings of L. S. Lowry*, London 1963

— *The Paintings of L. S. Lowry*, London 1975

oman, J., *American Primitive Painting*, New York, London 1942

— and Winchester, A., eds, *Primitive Painters in America 1750–1950*, New York 1950

tle, N. F., *Country Art in New England*, Sturbridge 1965

quet, G. H., *L'art primitif*, Paris 1930

argonari, Renzo, *Naïfs?* Parma 1973

éndez, Fernandez, *Les Primitif Haitiens*, Galerie Georges S. Nader, Port-au-Prince, 1972

onks Hall Museum, Eccles, *A Tribute to L. S. Lowry*, Eccles 1964

ullins, Edwin, *Alfred Wallis: Cornish Primitive Painter*, London 1967

useum of Modern Art, *Masters of Popular Painting: modern primitives of Europe and America*, New York 1938

oszlopy, George T., *The Primitive Art of Bryan Pearce*, London, 1964

rruchot, H., *Le douanier Rousseau*, Paris 1957

hribny, Arsen and Tkáč, Štefan, *Naïve Art in Czechoslovakia*, Prague 1967

ch, D. C., *Henry Rousseau*, New York 1946

odman, Selden, *Horace Pippin*, New York 1947

mon, A., *Henri Rousseau dit le douanier*, Paris 1927

upault, Philippe, *Henri Rousseau, le douanier*, Paris 1927

dow, E. von, *Primitive Kunst und Psychoanalyse*, Vienna 1927

evoz, Michel, *L'art brut*, Geneva 1975

áč, Štefan, ed., *Bratislava: Slovenskà Nàrodnà Galéria. Insitné umenie* (Naïve art: collection of reports and discussions contributed to the 1st and 2nd International Symposia on Naïve Art, 1966–69)

de, W., *Cinq maîtres primitifs*, Zurich 1947 (Paris 1949; Eng. trans, R. Thompson, New York 1949)

— *Henri Rousseau le douanier*, Paris 1911

— *Rousseau, le douanier*, Lausanne 1948

llejo-Nagera, Juan Antonio, *Naifs españoles contemporaneos*, Madrid 1975

llier, Dora, *Henri Rousseau*, Cologne 1961 (Eng. ed. 962)

lsecchi, M., *La pittura di Rosina Viva*, Milan 1952

nturi, L., *Il gusto dei primitivi*, Bologna 1926

erner, A., *Henri Rousseau*, New York 1957

esker, Arnold and Allin, John, *Say Goodbye, You May Never See Them Again*, London 1974

ilenski, R. H., *Douanier Rousseau 1844–1910*, London 953

illiams, Sheldon, *Voodoo and the Art of Haiti*, London 969

ingert, Paul S., *Primitive Art: its traditions and styles*, New York, 1962

rvos, Christian, *Rousseau*, Paris 1927

Catalogues

Exhibition catalogues are listed under the name of the painter in the case of individual exhibitions and under the name of the town where the exhibition was held in the case of general exhibitions

Amsterdam: Stedelijk Museum. De Grote Naïeven, 1974

Basle: Gewerbemuseum. Laienmaler, 1961

Bauchant, André
  Exhibition catalogues
    London: Lefèvre Gallery, 1938
    Paris: Galerie Charpentier, 1949
    Amsterdam: Stedelijk Museum, 1949
    London: Gimpel Fils, 1953
    Basle: Kunsthalle, 1956
    Tours: Musée des Beaux-Arts, 1960
    London: Mayer Gallery, 1969
    Zurich: Le Corbusier Galerie, 1975

Belgrade: Muzej Primenjene Umetnosti. VII dečji Oktobarski Salon primenjena umetnost, 1970

Bratislava: Slovenská Národná Galéria. Strelecké terče, 1972; Trienale insitného umenia, 1972

Dortmund: Museum am Ostwall, Maler des einfältigen Herzens, 1952

Durham, North Carolina: Duke University. Naïve Painters of Latin America, 1962

Frankfurt: Galerie Margo Ostheimer. Die Naïven Malerinnen von Uzdin, 1972

Hamburg: Altonaer Museum. Naïve Kunst der Gegenwart aus Polen: Gemälde, Aquarelle, Zeichnungen, Graphik, Stickiereien, Hinterglasbilder, Skulpturen, 1972

—— Naïve Kunst im Ruhrgebiet, 1971

Leningrad: Hermitage. Paintings and Sculpture by Primitive Artists of Yugoslavia, 1963

London: Circle Gallery. International Exhibition of Naïve Painting, 1967

London: Commonwealth Institute. Lancashire Primitive Paintings, 1972

London: Grosvenor Gallery. The Spontaneous Eye, II, 1968

London: Institute of Contemporary Arts. 40,000 Years of Modern Art, with an essay by W. G. Archer and R. Melville and preface by Herbert Read

London: South London Art Gallery. Northern Primitives, 1972

—— Primitive Art from Poland, 1968

London: Tooth and Sons' Gallery. The "Naïf" Painters of Haiti, 1968 and 1969

—— Les Peintres Naïfs, III 1966; IV 1967; V 1968; VI 1969

—— South American Country Art: Paintings by Self-

Taught Artists from Brazil, Colombia and Honduras, 1970–71

Lowry, L. S.
  Exhibition catalogues from London
    Lefèvre Gallery in 1939, 1943 (with J. Herman), 1948 (with Barbara Hepworth), 1951, 1953, 1956, 1958, 1961, 1963, 1964, 1967, 1971
    Arts Council, 1966
    Crane Kalman Gallery, 1966–67
  Exhibition catalogues from galleries outside London
    Salford: City Art Gallery, 1951
    Manchester: City Art Gallery, 1959
    Sheffield: Graves Art Gallery, 1962
    Newcastle: Stone Gallery, 1964
    Norwich: Castle Museum, 1970

Lugano: Villa Ciani. I Naïfs; II Mostra internazionale dei pittori naifs, 1973

Manchester: City Art Gallery. Polish Primitive Art, 1969

Milan: Galleria Cortina. Naïfs Bali, 1972

Milan: Rotonda. La grande domenica: rassegna internazionale dei Naïfs, 1974

Munich: Haus der Kunst. Die Kunst der Naïven, 1974–5

New York: Hirschl and Adler Galleries. Plain and Fancy: a survey of American folk art, 1970

Ottawa: National Gallery of Canada. People's Art: naïve art in Canada, 1973–4

Paris: Exposition de "Beaux-Arts". Un siècle de peinture naïve, 1933 (preface by Raymond Cogniat)

Paris: Galerie des Quatre Chemins. Les peintres du Coeur Sacré, 1928

Paris: Grand Palais des Champs-Elysées. Peintres naïves américaines, 1968

Paris: Musée d'Art Moderne. Le monde des naïfs, 1964

Paris: Musée du Louvre. Les primitifs français, 1904

Prato: Palazzo Pretorio. Incontri con i pittori primitivi, 1971

Rio de Janeiro: Museu Nacional de Belas Artes, 1975

Rome: Ente Premi Roma. Pittori naïfs italiani e francesi, 1964

Rome: Palazzo Barberini. Naïfs a Roma, 1973

Rotterdam: Museum Boymans-van Beuningen. De Lusthof der Naïven, 1965

Rousseau, Henri
  Exhibition catalogues
    Paris: Bernheim-Jeune and Co.'s Gallery, 1912
    Berne: Kunshalle, c. 1936
    Paris: Paul Rosenberg Gallery, 1937
    New York: Museum of Modern Art, 1942
    Paris: Galerie Charpentier, 1961
    New York: Guggenheim Museum, 1968

Salzburg: Residenz. Die Welt der Naïven Malerei, 1964

Saskatoon: Mendel Art Gallery. Saskatchewan Primitives, 1975

Storrs, Conn.: University of Connecticut. Nineteen Century Folk Painting, 1973

Thun: Kunstsammlung der Stadt Thun. Naïve Mal 1971

Utrecht: Centraal Museum. Albert Dorne collectie naïeve schilderkunst

Vienna: Österreichisches Museum für angewan Kunst. Peintres naïfs: amerikansiche Volksamale von 1670 bis heute, 1954

Vivin, Louis
  Exhibition catalogues
    Paris: Galerie Bing, 1948
    New York: Perls Galleries, 1954 and 1967
    Basle: Kunsthalle, 1956

Warsaw: Polska Akademia Nauk. Polish Peasant A 1968

Washington: National Gallery of Art. 101 Americ Primitive Water Colors and Pastels from the Collecti of Edgar William and Bernice Chrysler Garbisch, 19

West Point: United States Military Academy. Americ Naïve Painting from the Collection of Colonel a Mrs Edgar Garbisch, 1970

Winterthur: Kunstverein Museum. Naïve Malerei Ungarn 1900–71, 1972

Zagreb: Jugoslavenska Akademija Znanosti i Umjetno Naïve Art in Yugoslavia Today, 1963

Articles

Note The principal journal on primitive art is *Insita* articles in it are not listed individually. Its full title *Insita: Bulletin of Insite Art*, published by the publish house Obzor for the Slovak National Gallery, Bratisla Czechoslavakia. It commenced publication in 1971 a was edited by Štefan Tkáč. Contributions devoted naïve and primitive art appeared simultaneously Czech, Russian, French and English.

L'Arte Naivi, published 3 times yearly in Reggio Emi deals only with naïve art

Ambron, E., Rapporti fra l'arte primitiva e gli art europei, *Realtà nuova* 4:310–11, 1953

Argan, G. C., Dell'idea dei "primitivi" nella sto dell'arte, *Arch. di filosofia* I: 91–7, 1953

Bihalji-Merin, Oto, Primitive Masters from Near a Far, *Graphis* 18: 336–51, May 1962

Bing-Bodmer, H., Lettre sur Louis Vivin, *Du* XII, 2:21 1952

Blasdel, G. N., Grass Roots Artist, *Art In America* 24–41, September 1968

Bock, J., Grand Pa Wiener, Painter of Many Wor *Antiques* 98:266–9, August 1970

Brosi, C., Ernst Reisemey, ein Schweizerischer Sonnta maler, *Werk* 43:234–6, July 1956

ampbell, W. P., Amateurs, Frakturs and Elegant Young Ladies, *Art News*, 65:50-3, October 1966

assou, J., Les maîtres populaires de la réalité, *Art vivant* 201-3, 1937

—— Les primitifs du XXe siècle au Musée d'Art Moderne, *Musées de France* 169-71, August 1948

ogniat, R., Shalom of Safed, an Israeli Watchmaker Paints Biblical Stories, *Graphis* 18:516-23, September 1962

ooper, D., Henri Rousseau: artiste-peintre, *Burlington Magazine* 85:158, 160-5, July 1944

escargues, P., Louis Vivin et trois siècles de peinture à la Galerie Bing, *Arts, Beaux-Arts, Littérature, Spectacles* 5, March 1948

orfles, G., L'arte dei primitivi contemporanei, *Domus* 379:534, June 1961

eppard, C. W., What is Primitive and What Is Not? *Antiques* 41:308-10, May 1942

avoisin, J., French Refugee Becomes a Swiss Peasant Painter, *Graphis* 22 no. 128:542-3, 1966

wight, E. H., Art in Early Cincinnati, *Cincinnati Art Museum Bulletin* new series 3:3-11, August 1953

exner, J. T. New Bottles for Old Wine: American artisan, amateur and folk paintings, *Antiques* 41:246-9, April 1942

ist, H. F., Die Laienmalerei und der Missbrauch des Naïven *Werk* 38:84-92, March 1951

ll, Madge, Interviews in *Prediction*, London 1937 and *Psychic News*, London 1942

ordon, A., Naïve Painting, *Connoisseur* 170:100, February 1969

raut, H., Le quincaillier mélomane, Vandersteen, *Arts, Beaux-Arts, Littérature, Spectacles* 1ff., July 1948

ernandez, A. and others, Naïve Kunst, *Werk* 48:393-404, November 1961

offman, E., Naïve Painters in Rotterdam and Paris, *Burlington Magazine* 106-473-4, October 1964

olzinger, H., Die Kundst der Naïven, Haus der Kunst, *Pantheon* 33:65-7, January 1975

uyghe, René, La peinture d'instinct, *L'amour de l'art* 14:185-8, 1933

ovsky, Anatole, Le douanier Rousseau savait-il peindre? *Médicine de France* no. 218, 1971

affroy, A., L'inspiration populaire, *Domus* 404:44-6, July 1963

y, E. T., Early Pioneering Days in the Australian Outback: some original drawings in a London collection, *Connoisseur* 164:170-5, March 1967

nnedy, D. S., Slinging Paint, *Design* 49:19ff., January 1948

nnedy Galleries, American Primitives: primitive, folk and naïve arts from the 18th, 19th and 20th centuries, *The Kennedy Quarterly* IX:iii, 1969

Lambert, M. and Marx, E., English Primitive Painting, *Antiques* 57:350-4, May 1950

Lévêque, J. J., Huit peintres naïfs brésiliens: exposition à Paris, *Aujourd'hui* 9:28, April 1965

Levy, Mervyn, Scottie Wilson's Kingdom in Kilburn, *Studio* no. 830, 1962

Lipman, J., Eunice Pinney: an early Connecticut watercolorist, *Art Quarterly* 6, no.3:213-21, 1943

Little, N. F., New Light on Joseph H. Davis, "Left-Hand Painter", *Antiques* 98:754-7, November 1970

Luzzato, G., Una curiosa polemica contra la moda dei primitivi nel 1824, *Comm.* XI:87-90, 1960

Meyer, F., Primitive im 20 Jarhundert, *Du* XII, 2:6-18, 1952

Michelson, A., Modern Primitives at the Maison de la Pensée Française, *Arts* 35:21, November 1960

Murray, G., In Search of Naïves, *Arts and Artists* 5:16-19, December 1970

Nacenta, R., Bauchant le Tourangeau, *L'Oeil* nos. 221-2: 52-9, December 1973—January 1974

Nemser, C., Three Primitive Pennsylvanians: Hicks, Kane, Pippin, *Arts Magazine* 40:30-2, September 1966

Pierre, J., Raphaël Lonné et le retour des médiums, *L'Oeil* 216:30-43, December 1972

Previtali, G., Collezionisti di primitivi nel Settecento, *Paragone* X, 113:3-32, 1959

—— La controversia secentesca sui "primitive", *Paragone* X, 119:3-28, 1959

—— Le prime interpretazioni figurate dai "primitive", *Paragone* XI, 121:15-23, 1960

Réau, L., Les primitifs de la collection Dard au musée de Dijon, *La Gazette des Beaux-Arts*, series 6, vol. 2:335-56, supp. 3-4, December 1929

—— Quelques remarques sur les primitifs des écoles suisses et allemandes dans la collection Dard à Dijon, *ibid.*, series 6, vol. 5:94-102, supp. 2, February 1931

Restany, P., Un mystère à la mode: le monde des naïfs, *Domus* 42:23, 28-9, February 1965

Rham, D. de, L'art brut à Lausanne, *L'Oeil* 249:22-7, April 1976

Roditi, E., Prophet in Berlin: F. Schroeder Sonnenstern, *Arts* 31:224, February 1957

Roh, F., Das naïve Bild der Welt; Austellung in Baden-Baden, *Das Kunstwerk* 15:28-33, September 1961

—— Henri Rousseau Bildform und Bedeutung fuer die Gegenwart, *Die Kunst fuer Alle*, XLII:105-14, 1927

Rumford, B., Nonacademic English Painting, *Antiques* 105:336-75, February 1974

Schurr, G. Jean Kwiat and an Enchanted World, *Connoisseur* 182:114-16, February 1973

—— Paris in Search of Naïveté, *Connoisseur* 158:50, January 1965

Seckler, D., Success of Mrs Moses, *Art News* 50:28–9, May 1951

Seddon, R., Artists of Note: S. J. L. Birch, *Artist* 27:86–8, June 1944

Taylor, G. and others, Grass Roots Art in Canada, *Arscanada* 26:4–35, December 1969

Turner, E. H., Toward an Appreciation and Understanding of "primitive art", *Canadian Art* 20:163–7, May 1963

Uhde, W., Henri Rousseau et les primitifs modernes, *L'amour de l'art*, XIV:189–94, 1933

Vallier, Dora, Les peintres naïfs bulgares, *L'Oeil* 245: 50–1, December 1975

Venturi, L., Art populaire et art primitifs, *Actes XI. Cong. int. d'h. de l'art* Brussels, I:333–6, 1930

Verillon, P., Le palais idéal du facteur Cheval, *Gazette d Beaux-Arts* series 6, vol. 76:159–84, September 1970

Watt, A., La peinture naïve français du douanier Rousse. à nos jours at the Maison de la Pensée Française, *Stud* 160:105–7, September 1960

—— Nouveaux naïfs; contemporary primitives, *Art America* 51:91–2, April 1963

Webster, J. C., Junius R. Sloan, Self-Taught Arti *Art in America* 40 no. 3:103–52, 1952

Zanzi, E., Un autodidatta: Vittorio Risso, *Emporir* 94:231, November 1941